overthinking

the psychology of me (and maybe others)

Ryhan Clarke

Overthinking – the psychology of me (and maybe others)

Dedication

I have downloaded a book template which according to the layout, suggests that it is at this point that I have to dedicate this book to someone and provide the reasons as to why.

The problem with determining who to dedicate anything to requires a significant amount of thought, especially if you are trying to steer away from the conventional types e.g. my wife, my, children, my mother, my father, my partner, my brother, my sister, my grandfather, my grandmother, my uncle, my auntie, my cousin, my dog etc etc, you get the point.

So as I am determined to break convention, I am therefore dedicating this book to Floela Benjamin on the basis that whilst trying to think of someone from a leftfield position, she, for whatever reason popped into my mind. It wasn't even Playschool that I went to first, it was just Floela Benjamin direct. Now I'm trying to think of a reason to properly dedicate this book to her, and quite frankly I'm doing this from memory as opposed to trawling through the internet. So, from memory and considering the accolades that she has, I am dedicating it to her because of her early television work that she did to entertain and educate and inspire a generation. I think she also received and MBE or something of this ilk which also warrants why she is worthy of this dedication.

For anyone who does not know who Floela Benjamin is, I would suggest that you do some research, alternatively think of that guy Andy from CBeebies and imagine him receiving an OBE.

To this end, I thank you Floela for helping me allow significant content to tackle the challenge of writing a dedication, which has not only meant that I have filled a complete page, but I have also moved away from the conventional cliché approach, whilst additionally allowing written evidence as to how it is indeed possible to go off track.

I have also just realised that it could have just been; For Floela (Andy), an inspiration. This would have also sufficed, although given who they are, the appropriate context probably makes a difference, especially for those that are unaware of either individual.

If you do not know who Floela Benjamin or Andy are, I don't really know what to say. It might be that you substitute them for someone that you do know, although what I would say is that you should choose someone that you know, but you only for an obscure reason. This way my dedication makes much more sense. It is conceivable that you might know who Floela Benjamin and Andy are, but are not obscure enough for you, so equally you could substitute them for other people as well. I won't make any suggestions; this is something you should do of your own accord.

Table of Contents

Foreword

As per my previous entry, as this is a template that I am working from, I am being informed by said template that in this section that the following should be adhered: *'Replace this wording with your own foreword. A foreword is written by somebody other than the author, and usually tells of some interaction between the writer of the foreword and the author during the writing of the book. Also, be sure to spell "foreword" properly. When it is a part of a book, as it is here, it's spelled "Foreword". When it's a direction of travel, it's spelled "Forward". If you don't have a foreword, simply delete this entire page'*.

The latter part of this advice is ridiculous on the basis that if you didn't know the difference between 'foreword' and 'forward', at least from a spelling perspective, it would be questionable as to whether writing a book was something that you should aspire to do. Whilst this might sound a bit patronising, I also equally admit that if asked before reading this free template, my response would have been that I don't actually know. At a guess I would have probably said something about a section or portion of an excerpt from the book that was supposed to set the scene. Either that or a mini-introduction. As per said template advice, it is now clear as to what it should be.

Allowing for this, I have considered this actual definition of 'foreword' and continuing my determination to break from convention, I have decided to write the following foreword myself, to myself, about the interaction that I have had with myself.

I met with myself regularly and the interaction that I had was very useful in helping to determine what the book would be about and how the book would be developed. The upshot of all of this meant that it allowed for good discussions with myself, and although there were lots of arguments, crucially we were always there for one another. It goes without saying that the ability to do this was key to all this writing taking place.

Preface

'Replace this wording with your own. A preface follows the foreword, and is written by the author, and generally describes how the book was developed. If you don't have a preface, simply delete this entire page.'

It appears that I have done this via the foreword, however I do like a challenge and through further elaboration, I believe a preface is warranted.

Following on from my earlier provision of facts covering the interaction that I had with myself, I would like to add further information as to how this book was developed. Basically, the actual construct of the book was, and has been in my thought process for a long time. It is through now having a period of time away from work that I am able to apply myself. I have made a conscious decision to make good use of my downtime by being proactive and not to just sit around watching 15-minute YouTube videos for the entire summer, whilst cursing my own laziness, only stopping through my hand turning numb through carpal tunnel syndrome.

So, unlike any previous thoughts or lackluster efforts that have been made in my pursuit of becoming an author, through copious amounts of walking my dog and a bit of application and planning, I am now committed to embarking on writing. Whether this will end up being any good is another matter, the main thing is that unlike my other failed attempts, I am further on than I have been before. At this stage, I would like to thank the template in assisting me in this work. It really is quite a splendid aid.

Desiderata

GO PLACIDLY amid the noise and the haste, and remember what peace there may be in silence. As far as possible, without surrender, be on good terms with all persons.

Speak your truth quietly and clearly; and listen to others, even to the dull and the ignorant; they too have their story.

Avoid loud and aggressive persons; they are vexatious to the spirit. If you compare yourself with others, you may become vain or bitter, for always there will be greater and lesser persons than yourself.

Enjoy your achievements as well as your plans. Keep interested in your own career, however humble; it is a real possession in the changing fortunes of time.

Exercise caution in your business affairs, for the world is full of trickery. But let this not blind you to what virtue there is; many persons strive for high ideals, and everywhere life is full of heroism.

Be yourself. Especially do not feign affection. Neither be cynical about love; for in the face of all aridity and disenchantment, it is as perennial as the grass.

Take kindly the counsel of the years, gracefully surrendering the things of youth.

Nurture strength of spirit to shield you in sudden misfortune. But do not distress yourself with dark imaginings. Many fears are born of fatigue and loneliness.

Beyond a wholesome discipline, be gentle with yourself. You are a child of the universe no less than the trees and the stars; you have a right to be here.

And whether or not it is clear to you, no doubt the universe is unfolding as it should. Therefore be at peace with God, whatever you conceive Him to be. And whatever your labors and aspirations, in the noisy confusion of life, keep peace in your soul. With all its sham, drudgery and broken dreams, it is still a beautiful world. Be cheerful. Strive to be happy.

By Max Ehrmann © 1927
(poster on bedroom wall 1993-1999)

Introduction

I have wanted to write a book for a considerable amount of time. I am 42 now and I believe that I first thought about doing this when I turned 30. As to the reasons why, I guess there are many; ranging from some innate feeling that I must make an attempt to show my creative side, whilst also appealing to my inner ego and the belief that people might be interested in what I have to say, to a desire to document something that resembles something close to a legacy. The idea of dying and not having at least tried to put something down in writing, leaves me with this idea that people might miss the opportunity to really know what or why I think the way I do. If, and it's a big if, that I do finish this book, at the very least I can go to the grave having splurged my bullshit and that would be absolutely fine by me, job done so to speak. Here you go great great grandchildren, look at me, look at me.

In terms of what this book is about, part of the reason why I am now able to put pen to paper is that my original idea was always based on writing my own autobiography which I have reconciled is something that I am unable to do. The problem with writing an autobiography is that what becomes abundantly clear very early on when trying to do it, is that unless you are willing to be completely honest about the things that you are writing about, you end up censoring yourself through the fear of revealing something that is probably best left alone. It is really a question as to how cathartic you want to go and how much you are willing to divulge which renders the real challenges that an autobiography brings. Equally, there is also a nagging doubt as to who really cares as to what you have to say? I think given the information that people are willing to part with is generally related to either a confirmation as to what people may already know about an individual, coupled with who the individual is, as to how comfortable they are in sharing personal details of their life and inner thoughts. I guess what I am trying to say is that given the personal nature of those inner secrets that we retain for ourselves, the ability to share these should be measured against the reasons as to what you are attempting to achieve. What is the point of telling someone that you wear your wife's underwear if nobody really gives a shit or is helped by the sharing of this information?

Whilst it is true that a book can be written for any reason at all, I believe (and this is where my current thinking is), that when writing non-fiction, there should be a purpose behind it to at least try to appeal to the reader. In my case, the purpose behind this book is to merely share my thoughts on a bunch of random topics to reach out and possibly find conformity or agreement in my beliefs. This is all based on an ongoing battle to address my problem of overthinking and the challenges that this brings to my life. I have arrived at the conclusion that to dissect this fully, through exploring this in more detail I might be able to make sense as to why I have this affliction and how it contributes towards my experiences in life. I am very much aware that this might sound either oversimplified or overdramatic, however the older that I get, through the pursuit of being content, there is a realisation that it is important to try and address or at least confront those things that are getting in the way of enjoying life to the full.

I have therefore decided that this book is my own self help book which I hope firstly allows me to put as much stuff down as possible, whilst hoping to receive feedback that either confirms I am a bit mental, confirms I am not mental, or confirms that I am either good at writing or bad at writing, and a little bit mental. Either way, I would like to think that through sharing my thoughts, the end result will be that at the very least somebody (one person), might like it. If they don't then it matters not, they can go and write their own fucking book about their own bollocks.

So anyway, this book is about me trying to write a book and lobbing in whatever comes into my mind as I try to make sense and exploring a number of subjects. I will try to make this coherent, although it is extremely likely that it won't be.

The end of the beginning

I apologise in advance as it appears that as predicted I have already begun to have doubts as to my ability to provide enough relevant material to keep people interested. You see, the biggest problem with setting out to achieve any type of goal is often paved with doubt and ultimately if this grows it can quite easily turn into 'fuck it I can't be arsed'. As to why this occurs, for me, it is often due to a lack of confidence or self-belief in the thing that I am doing.

It is here where what I consider to be a good idea begins to manifest into a mildly okay idea and then descends into a shit idea. I do find this particularly disheartening as for anyone who wishes to be creative, often it is this first obstacle that determines whether anything actually happens. I am undoubtedly my own biggest fan and my biggest critic, so I end up in this vicious circle which consists of an internalised debate where I either think I am utterly amazing, or by contrast, an absolute twat. Whilst I never really want to give in to the latter sentiment, the reality is that I am susceptible or likely to give up through what I can only describe as a 'middle voice' which essentially just tells me not to bother. It is at this point where I then will go back to the drawing board as to trying to consider what I might embark on next, however, this in itself is often circular as my efforts are generally consigned to the following;

Writing – drawing – podcasting – writing – drawing – podcasting.

So, basically there is something that I do want to do, but try as I might, for the reasons outlined above, the sad reality is that when it comes down to evidential achievements, I am somewhat limited to the sum of achieving fuck all, with the exception arguably of a few things that were only achieved because they required minimum effort.

Crucially, and because of my negative experiences, it has become abundantly clear because of the high number of failed attempts that the only way to see anything like this through is to persevere, albeit the challenge becomes about distancing yourself from any nagging doubts that you might have, and crucially making sure that you do something, even if indeed this 'something' runs the risk of being shite.

The bigger question though, and assuming this is true of others that feel compelled to undertake these extracurricular activities, is why? What is it that our lives fail to provide us where it necessitates a desire to pursue these interests?

We live in an age where more than ever where we are subjected to what other people are achieving, by this I refer to the over exposure of social media that both consciously and subconsciously leaves us questioning whether what we are doing is on par with everyone else? Whilst it is true that some people are less susceptible to being influenced by this, certainly older generations, or those that have chosen not to delve into it, the point remains that the longer this becomes the 'new normal' we become subjected to feel that we must be doing something greater than whatever it is we are actually doing. Obviously, there are levels to this depending on what it is that a person is doing as standard e.g., Bear Grylls fucking kayaking down Everest on a kite, but for most 'normal' people trapped in the mundanity of a 9-5 job, there is this pressure where we are left asking the question 'Am I doing enough?'

I know that this is an overgeneralisation as I am sure lots of people would suggest they don't relate to this, claiming that their lives are enriched by whatever they are doing, however if you consider this; if the response is that you believe you are achieving the 'extra' in your life, is it because you really are, or have you managed to convince yourself that you are because you are constantly promoting whatever it is that you are doing? Obviously, I can only speak for myself, but any contentment I have found by pursuing other activities is often promoted by me, telling others exactly that of which I am doing by whatever means I can to bring extra value to it. This sounds a little narcissistic, however I am convinced this is something again that we are all guilty of doing to greater or lesser degrees. I don't think however that it is done for any other reason but to generally fit in, almost showing undertones of competitiveness with those that we frequent with, often becoming some sort of modern game of Top Trumps.

'Went to the zoo with family, (8) vs went to the fucking Serengeti with family and was mauled by a lion, (10)'.

Essentially, we have migrated from what has commonly been referred to as 'Keeping up with the Joneses ', something that was often limited to the proximity of family, close friends, and neighbours, to a much larger scale, again influenced heavily by our exposure to social media and what is the overzealous use of self-PR. Given the sheer volume of what we are exposed to, it is easy to therefore understand why people have such insecurities as to why they might feel so inept when comparing themselves to others, which it has to be said is infinitely made worse when you come across those people purportedly achieving success that you immediately consider to be unfair, either due to that fact that you believe they have been given certain advantages that for whatever reason is not available to you, or, that you simply think that those receiving these advantages are simply massive twats. Often it is a combined mixture of both these things.

It might be that we commonly associate this with the world of celebrity, which is the obvious easy target, especially given how this is seemingly become so normalised and reflected in younger generations who now actively seek this out as an active career option. This should not however be underestimated as the longer-term implications are that there is a threat of an increasingly dissatisfied society with a number of people becoming even more unhappy with the jobs that they find themselves in (something that has often been the case anyway), yet it is somewhat now amplified by what appears to be much easier routes towards the career of celebrity. Consider the words 'Influencer' 'YouTuber' and 'TikTokker', 20 years ago, these vocations never existed, yet here we are. Forget about what we were told as to what the internet would bring us, as of now, this (among other shite), is the culmination of humanities progress. We appear to have moved on from 70% plus of internet traffic being pornography, to this. This is our epic progress towards utopian enlightenment.

I am fully aware that I have gone off topic, but there is a point that I am trying to make which is merely to suggest that in terms of the desire to be not just creative, but also have some sort of meaning to our lives, the fact is that we now have greater access to being able to do this, certainly with regards to being creative. When this is coupled with the fact that we are now subjected daily to millions of people utilising technology to show their own creativity, and shit they are doing, it all adds further weight to greater levels of inadequacy in our own miserable efforts to join in. I'm not saying that we all should have a desire to enter the world of social media seeking out Z list celebrity status etc, however I do think that the more exposed we are to what other people are doing, this can leave us questioning our own ineffectiveness when it comes to registering our own achievements.

Again, this is not to say that this is necessarily a new phenomenon, however it is exacerbated by how we perceive the achievements of others because we are constantly surrounded by it. Whilst it is true that we can certainly distance ourselves from it, in terms of making a concerted effort to reduce or refrain from subscribing to social media, the reality is that by and large is still not enough as this has become so mainstream that it is everywhere we go. I'm not suggesting that this is a debilitating world ending issue, although I do think that whether we like it or not, there is a societal shift that is putting more pressure on people to not only want to seek out personal development, but in doing so they want to, or feel inclined to make sure everyone fucking knows about it.

I'm trying to be honest, certainly when it comes to my own feelings of inadequacy. Whilst I am comfortable or happy with any achievements that I have made, I guess the discernable difference is that I am left with a feeling that these have only happened due to the circumstances that I have found myself in, as opposed to actively gaining achievements for something that I personally wanted to do.

As melodramatic as this sounds and conceding that clearly this is not true of all people, given that there will be those that have set goals and have indeed pursued their 'dreams' so to speak, with regards to my own experiences and others that that I either frequent with or know, I would argue that this is something that is mainly exclusive to the minority of people. If anything, it is exactly for this reason that I think there has been this shift towards people who possibly feel that they have not had the opportunity to pursue things that they are interested in, and now with greater means to now do this as evidenced by those that are, there is now possibly more pressure to feel that we should be doing more.

So, we now have the tools that we often said the absence of prevented us from doing more, so by default the excuses for not doing these things now probably says more about us just being lazy bastards than anything else.

Somehow, I have managed to ramble on, which I think (or hope), has allowed me to set this book in motion which to a certain extent means that I am firmly on this journey. What I have decided to do in order to stay on course is to limit my re-reading of what I have written to get to this point. This is important as I know that were I to do this, I simply would have given up by now as I would have concluded early that I can neither write coherently, and whatever I am saying is nonsensical bullshit. Whilst this is undoubtedly true on both accounts, to see this project through, I must subscribe to utter ignorance of my own work. I will save the contempt for myself when I am finished.

As of now, I will have to assume that the first chapter has brought some enlightenment to whoever has read this far, possibly resonating in parts with the frustrations that I have had with wanting to do something but not quite being able to muster the effort or energy to do it. I appreciate that I have possibly repeated myself considerably, using different words to say the same thing. And in doing so probably alienated anyone making the effort to read this.

Regardless, it has become apparent that it is important to essentially just write lots of shit and where possible try to make it fit. I am using Microsoft Word and its tools to help set myself little targets.

As of now for example, given all of the words that I have typed, I am being reliably informed that this totals 4233 words. I don't actually know if this is a good amount, or it is considerably under for what this type of book should be. All I do know is that if I use the template, it suggests that the total amount of pages that I should use is 293+. I will therefore just assume this to be my target and stick to this.

As for this chapter though, this will just have to do for now, fuck it.

Nostalgic Bliss

There is something about reflecting on the past that the older we get, the more profound it becomes in how we use it to define us. What I mean by this is that anecdotally, depending on when you grew up, we find ourselves often referencing a period that we almost lay claim to owning. It is as if this has become the marker for one generation to use against another as some sort of veiled attempt of dominance over the other with the notion that 'our time was better than yours, so bow to our greatness'.

The fascinating aspect of the lure of nostalgia is that it is not something that you necessarily seek out, it tends to occur effortlessly and unintentionally as we age. It is a change of familiarity in the things that we have become accustomed to having in our lives and what impact they have on us, suddenly results in having greater importance in what they mean to us. In many ways it is only through the transition of change that what we view those things that we have taken for granted, now stand out as being considered as better than whatever the new alternatives are; especially if the new alternatives are really really shit. It is worth noting though that this is not something that occurs at the exact moment in time where something has become obsolete, it is only really when we reflect on the differences, where we then determine (often with fondness), how better things were before we had no or little choice but to embrace whatever new alternative is now available to us. The above is a protracted definition of 'Big Yellow Taxi'.[1]

As of now, and I imagine certainly for the foreseeable future, nostalgia to me is very much deep rooted in both the 1980's and 90's and this is because given my age it is these decades that are the embodiment of my time growing up, and it is this that I believe drives how we perceive nostalgia, which is why, or how it is used by one generation or age group to unite against another as to why their experiences are superior to others.

There is a reason that nostalgia is cemented in the experiences of youth, which is because the window is limited to a specific group of people that can identify with it. This is especially pertinent if we consider nostalgia to be a sort of club, the membership of said club is restricted merely by the time we happen to have been born. This is not to say that people who happen to have not been born in said time are not free to explore this period, although with the greatest of respect, these 'people' will never be embraced by a collective certified group of people, those that now exist in a club that's members consider themselves to have lived through it. A sort of bizarre form of social distancing is then witnessed. Think any Vietnam film "You weren't there man, you weren't there". We are talking about

1 Nostalgic reference

full on nostalgia discrimination here, and currently there are no laws to protect against it. We are all nostaligists, nostalgiphobes and I imagine in the fullness of time this will be punishable by either death, excommunication or bolted on to the Equal Opportunities Act 2010.[2]

What should be considered though is that whilst any entry to a specific period of nostalgia is limited by when we are born e.g., *after the date = you shit out*, it is worth pointing out that this is also restricted to those that were also born too early but did live through it. An example might be that if you happen to have entered the world in the 1940's, and although you would have lived through the 80's and 90's, there is a preclusion of said people due to the fact that they are deemed to be ignorant to what constitutes as what was nostalgic for this time. To be blunt, the feeling is there is no way that these 'people' appreciate those things that have become synonymous for these times, although the irony is that it was this very same group of people that were responsible for giving us the things that we identify as being unique to these times.

Nonetheless, regardless of this fact, even though they bear the responsibility for giving us the things that we hold dear to our hearts, by virtue of them not having the same experiences that we had, are considered to have merely just 'been there' and were not partaking in any of the 'actual fun' that the rest of us had. It is irrelevant that they might have a better degree of knowledge or retained memory of

2 Or any other countries equivalent legislation

said time, but ultimately the fact remains that how they recall The A-Team, Knightrider and BMX bikes is very different to how a person of youth at this time remember it. That is the real difference, and it applies for every generation when considering what constitutes as nostalgic for any given period of time that people are referring to.

Additionally, the reason I want to talk about nostalgia is that it does tie into the theme of the book in terms of it being problematic towards any pursuits that we try to take on as we get older. Not with regards I'm to anything new that we are doing, but that of which we try to recapture or emulate from any past ventures. Nostalgia is very much engrained in us referring to the achievements that we have previously made, and by default this somehow becomes a benchmark that we then apply future standards to. This is most common when we find ourselves reminiscing with close friends where conversations often revert to past glories, where we find ourselves effectively boasting about anything that we have badged as an accomplishment that we achieved yesteryear. Certainly, within my circle of friends, the older we have become, it is almost guaranteed that through any gathering that takes place, it doesn't take long for any conversation to move firmly into the territory of 'remember this, remember when I did that.....'

Don't get me wrong, it is fair to say that there is a significant proportion of this that revolves around many of the embarrassing aspects of youth, however, equally there is a lot of self-congratulatory and affirmation given towards other areas, which often centers around sporting achievements amongst other things. What actually takes place though, regardless of any discussions around that which we probably would rather forget, is that we are left with a collection of stories that somehow have defined who we once were, which is then held in contrast against who we have later become. When we repeat these conversations (and we really fucking do), it suggests that as a group of friends, we see this as some sort of comfort blanket or something that we would prefer to identify with over anything that we have done in later life, or at the least, the fact that we identify with this period of time collectively is because this was something that we all experienced almost as 'one'. It is more that the value of the shared experience (albeit made up of individual stand out moments), take precedence over whatever we are doing now. I think this is because the natural order once you reach a certain age, is that where previously there was a greater chance of 'shared experiences', this changes significantly as people begin to venture out and take their own paths as to the next steps of life.

There can be a number of reasons as to why this happens, yet more often than not it will be because of either a career or a relationship. In both cases, these break the mould of the joint chronological events of what was experienced, and once this occurs the trajectory of people's lives will normally differ; sometimes to the point where the differences mean that the only thing left that people have in common with one another is limited to their shared past experiences. This is not necessarily a bad thing, in as much that when this happens it is confirmation that we have moved on and not necessarily subjected to the same peer pressure or comparisons that influence us at a younger age.

As outlined above, I am mindful of how some of this might come across, and unequivocally I am not saying that the lure of nostalgia detracts from any more recent life experiences or achievements that have had a profound effect on us; such as getting married, having children, going on Center Parcs holidays etc, however I would repeat my earlier point that these achievements are in essence considered as the 'natural order of life', and therefore certainly to others, (especially those that have also done these things) as less unique to what we achieved before. Categorically, these are significant and amazing life changing moments and I am not necessarily saying that scoring a 30 yard goal against a 38 year old postman necessarily is a greater achievement than becoming a Father, getting married, or indeed going to Center Parcs etc, my point is that these moments in life on face value, are just something that we have naturally come to do, and it is by proxy of the fact that there are lots of people doing these things, that say what you want, but that 30 yard goal against that 38 year old postman is still unique to the individual and thus renders this achievement as monumental.

Fuck me, those last few pages were difficult to write, I hope that it makes sense. I guess the crux of what I am saying, is to offer an explanation as to why, or how nostalgia plays into the mindset and the reasons for it. I think there is an argument to be had as to the link between shared experiences vs individual experiences which I believe offers some understanding as to why or how nostalgia can impact us. A shared experience, just purely based on numbers, will result in a specific period of time having greater significance and understandably warrant greater attention.

I suppose the bigger aspect which I want to highlight is depending on a person's view, or experiences based on a certain timeframe (something that will have been attributed certain nostalgic values), can influence any current or future endeavours that we might have. As individuals we are shaped by our experiences and never is this truer than when we have actually achieved something. This very much plays into the notion of 'living on past glories', and again this can have an impact as to how this affects us in our lives. In most cases it is fair to say that when we achieve, it can act as a driver towards betterment, certainly from a psychological perspective. Again, with regards to a 'natural order', this is something that we need in our lives so that we can start to apply our own standards, which should mean that we develop towards the place where we want to be. Certainly, if we can apply a level, or points scheme to an achievement e.g., PB at a running distance or a grade in an exam paper, in these instances the opportunity to 'achieve again' is somewhat more realistic as we are dealing with our own standards and benchmarks. I would go as far to say that this can be something that works, providing that you are motivated and use this as an opportunity or as a method of improving yourself.

Here lies the problem though, and again this is an example which also relates to the subject area of nostalgia. You see, if we consider the earlier parts of our lives, we are conditioned by the environment that we are in, where we were found to be constantly challenging ourselves which was manifested through our education. The entire focus within our time at school centers on achievement throughout, so in terms of choice, whilst even at a young age we could still show apathy or reluctance to participating towards gaining achievements, the reality is that like it or not, we are somewhat living in an environment that lays out a level of expectancy on everything that we are doing, and not only that, but we are participating in this with many others in the same position. So, if we then consider this period of time, it is likely because of these conditions that we find that we probably achieved more here than at other points in our life. This is not necessarily 'peak achievements', but the volume of what is achieved is certainly higher as the environment we were in, almost demanded it from us.

Some people might question how true this is, especially those that have made great efforts to live their lives by setting themselves high standards to continue to achieve, however the key difference is that the onus is much more on the individual where they make a conscious decision that this is something that they want to do, as opposed to having these set for us by others who expect us to be doing everything that we can to do achieve.

You could argue that to a degree that in our working lives this is an extension of mandatory expectations, especially where there is either a demand from the business or the employee to improve upon their position, yet the point (which is what I alluded to earlier), is that this often is much more related to an individual and not a collective group. This therefore supports the notion that although it is still an important part of what we achieve in our life, it sits outside what might be considered as 'nostalgic' as it is an isolated event that only we took part in.

I would like to think that I have not rambled on too much and that I have set my points out as to the effect that nostalgia can have on us with regards to why we return to it and why it can prevent us from doing more. I say this because on the basis that we refer to a period more affectionally than others, we do so because it represents what we determine to be when we were at our best, represented by what we achieved during this time and importantly we reflect this through others that had similar experiences. The downside is that unless we are personally motivated and driven, the less we achieve in later life which only makes this period even more important, as regardless of whether or not we do anything again, we can still refer to this time and recall exactly what we did do, hence creating a vicious circle where if anything, we are inclined to become even more nostalgic.

So, all in all, fundamentally despite my overelaboration of this subject, I don't think nostalgia is a bad thing, but it can be if given too much credence. As a positive, it can be an opportunity for people to come together and share their memories which in itself is particularly useful for when we do catch up with friends that we have had for years. The ability to be nostalgic in these circumstances allows for a level of solidarity or understanding as to why people remain as close as they are. This is especially poignant where friendships are strong, as while we are unable to escape from our past, we are given the opportunity to learn from it and in the absence of any mandatory challenges, it is through our relationship with our friends that it is possible to take on fresh challenges and create what might become 'new nostalgia' in years to come.

Ideally we should not let nostalgia have the negative effect by restricting our willingness to embark in new challenges. It should not be the case that simply because you have done something before that it should stop you from doing it again, as you will probably end up doing yourself a disservice and creating an excuse for not doing anything at all. This is the epitome of living on past glories.

$E = MC^2$

I have always been fascinated by time, which I think was born out of an early obsession with the movie Back to the Future; so much so that I became fixated with not only the idea of all things related to the past and present within my own world, but I also became almost romantically fixated on what the future might bring; somewhat holding on to a fantastical belief in the notion that it would retain elements of what was originally there, but ultimately it would be infinitely better. I do distinctly recall trying to build a time machine using an old record player that was dumped in a nearby ditch, but sadly to no avail. I am sure that if I had have had better twigs and greater confidence in banging magnets with stones, things could have been so much more different.

The appeal was always about being able to know that at some point I would bear witness to my ideological future, and this filled me with an air of excitement as to how things would change and what impact they would have. I think the reason that I felt this way was even at a young age I had this sense of optimism towards the future, which was driven by a desire for not only my life, but others to be better, based on the naive assumption that the future was always going to provide improvements on what we had. This is of course is my perspective on this now reflecting on how I like to think my young mind saw this, and as philosophical as it might sound, I have concluded that it is not actually that outlandish. Where most kids think about wishing to become a spaceman, fireman or footballer, this was my alternative version of this, I just wanted to 'be in the future'.

It is probably here where the origins of my overthinking took root; it was the start of an internalised battle to absorb as much information as I could, as I felt that this was an important element in making sense of the world and all that was in it. As to how this relates to time, I guess I saw it then (and still do now), that to fully appreciate why things are the way they are, it was vital to gain as much knowledge as possible. As to what type of knowledge, this was, and always has been very none specific, with the criteria predominantly based on what I was most likely able to retain and then recall when needed.

It might be that all of the above (minus the Back to the Future reference) is not wholly relevant to the subject matter, however I did want to mention this, as in many ways this has a bearing on how we use the time that we have. Our perception, or understanding of the world is significant as to the challenges that we face in living in it, or indeed our 'ability' or 'inability' to live in it. The fallacy that I have ultimately found, is that based on the following paradox of *'knowledge is power' and 'ignorance is bliss'*, the older I have got, I have come to fully prescribe to the latter, although unfortunately, given the lifetime pursuit of knowledge, it is far too late to suddenly adopt a lifestyle to accommodate this mindset and the benefits that it may bring.

The reality is that once you know something, it can be very difficult or impossible to unknow it. In some regards it could be argued that this is a good skill to have, especially for those circumstances where it is deemed to be beneficial, however, the problem depends mainly on the person that you are, it can be that the ability to 'filter' what might be deemed as useful information, over that which is not is hard to do. It can be somewhat problematic, especially where it takes you down various rabbit holes, which in real terms only provides you with additional information that in truth just adds to the uselessness. What I am referring to is really the issue with how much energy is sapped from you when you become trapped in the pursuit of gaining knowledge that has no relevance to anybody or anything.

At this juncture, mainly because as I type this, I concede (as with other stuff) that I am probably not managing to explain this properly, it therefore might be useful to provide some examples of the type of useless information that my brain has managed to retain over the years. In order to do this, I have decided to let my mind go to a number of places at random, in order to demonstrate the type of shit that I retain, whilst also possibly giving an insight as to my train of thought. So, here goes, here are 5 pieces of information that are fucking useless.

1. The TV show Minder, originally starred George Cole as Arthur Daley and his sidekick was played by Dennis Waterman, who played Terry. Subsequently after the show was cancelled, it was resurrected in the late 80's where the character of Terry was replaced by the character of Gary, after Dennis Waterman left. I don't know who played Gary.

2. If you take any page of writing, or read any label, say on a bottle of bleach, you will find that the letter 'e' is far more dominant than any other vowel in the collection of words, more often than not by about 25%. The letter 'a' is often a close second. This can be an effective way to pass time whilst not having a phone on the toilet. [3]

3. Staying on the subject of words, if you read words backwards, it can make you convincingly sound like a Warlock or a Witch recanting a spell.[4]

4. The boy who played Arnold in Different Strokes AKA Gary Coleman became a security guard after falling on hard times.

---

3 Count the e's vs a's and see the magic happen

4 Be careful

5. Bob Holness once played James Bond in a radio drama.

I must concede, that once I committed to coming up with 5 things to demonstrate my thought process, I then actually struggled to think at all. It was somewhat akin to when you think about the actions of breathing, where you suddenly start panicking, as for some reason your brain can't comprehend what comes after 'in'. The 5 on this list is therefore slightly contrived but still honest enough to provide a representation of both the so-called knowledge that I have, and how my brain operates.

The truth is that the word 'knowledge' should probably be switched out with the word 'bollocks', which would be far more appropriate as to what I actually consider to 'know', and based on the grandeur of the word 'knowledge', I think it is fair to say that the examples provided do not do justice to any of the dictionary definitions. If however, it is substituted with the word 'bollocks', and it is this offered in conversation, it would be far more becoming if the recipient of such 'bollocks', were to reply with 'hey man, you don't half know a lot of bollocks', as opposed to 'hey man, you have a lot of great knowledge'.

Here is the dilemma over the 'bollocks' element of this; at what point does giving information to someone about the TV show Minder, having 2 different characters called Terry and Gary, make any difference to the human race? At best, and I mean at fucking best, if a question were to come up in a pub quiz that just happened to be about the TV show 'Minder', and that question happened to be, 'what were the names of the 2 'Minders' in the TV show Minder?', then it could reasonably be argued that knowing that they were called Terry and Gary, might contribute towards the points score and help towards victory.

The above is quite literally the only real difference that knowing this would have. I mean you could possibly argue that if you were to take this to the extreme, and say that you happened to be held by terrorists, and in order to either save your own life or the life of others; if, and it's a massive fucking if, in order to survive you had to answer this question, then it could be quite useful here too.[5] Either that, or hope that your captors happen to be huge Minder fans and you can become friends with them by showing your brilliance and possibly agreeing to join forces and start up a 'Minder' fan club.

I think the above goes some way to offering an insight as to a demonstration of sorts, not only from being able to provide this information, but also as to some of the complexities in 'knowing' this information. I have no desire to retain these inane facts and yet here I am, trapped by them, luring me in with the temptation of pub quiz royalty, something that I don't even fucking partake in.

---

5 Not going to fucking happen

To get serious for a second, although I accept that people will generally retain lots of useless facts, I do genuinely think that for those that retain more, (and I am talking about the bollocks variety), once you take away the fun of the randomness of it, you are left with a sort of overload that inflates the inability to focus on the things that really matter. I think the way that I see it is that it almost gets in the way, and invariably leads you on a journey of further exploration into the world of bollocks, which only reduces the focus further.

Everything here though is about time, and particularly 'wasted time'. It is the way that our minds work that determine exactly what we 'do' or 'don't do' with the time that we have and how it is best (or badly) spent.

I don't mind admitting that this is a very difficult thing to write about, as on one hand despite being unable to filter information which renders me with pointless facts, equally, I do accept that having a thirst for knowledge does mean that through the passage of time, I have retained plenty of information that is valuable and is indeed worth sharing. It could simply be that in order to allow yourself the opportunity to become 'knowledgeable', it might be conditionally based on accepting that a high percentage of this has to be total bollocks in order for it to stick. I just don't know if this is true for other people or whether they see it the same way as I do?

The thing is though, I do still think that even with both the good and the bad, it all feels pretty redundant in the grand scheme of things. I mean this is probably the main crux of why I am trying to write this book, it's an attempt to try and give what I perceive to know meaning. The absence of application of what you know, only make what you know an even bigger waste of time than it already is.

The other factor, (and this is the real kicker), is that even when you subtract the bollocks elements of what you know, you are then essentially left with information that means you know about all that should in theory, matter. If in the context of the word 'matter', this includes all that is wrong with the world, you then know more and that results in you getting pissed off with this. I say pissed off, what I really mean is depressed as fuck about the state of things.

The counter argument would be to suggest that it is more depressing to be ignorant of the facts etc, however say what you like, but I've never come across an unhappy ignorant person. They tend to be both happy and angry at the same time[6]. I wouldn't mind a bit of that to be honest.

One of the realities of getting older is that the passage of time appears to go much quicker and this has become increasingly noticeable as years come and go. One of the key differences that we experience, is the somewhat regimented way that we live our lives. We tend to appear to recognise that in order to 'have order', this has to be the way or sequence that things are done. This relates in part

---

6 100% true

to what I previously referred to when discussing nostalgia; if you think about the period in your life where time seemed ageless, it is mainly because everything that you did on the face of it was the complete opposite of regimented. Anything that you had to do was so minimal that it meant that the time that you did have, allowed you to do more with it. This is why school holidays went on for fucking ages.

Again, I know that some people may not believe this to be true, however, I would argue that sadly for the majority of people, that it is. The deal with getting older is that we will have greater responsibilities, and in order to meet these, we have to commit our time towards all of the areas that require it. I'm not just referring to the duties of having to go to work, it goes much further than this. If this means as a result that we end up just repeating ourselves, it is no wonder that years go by so quickly, as there are less variance in our lives and it is precisely that which allows us to fully appreciate the times that we have.

I can imagine that some people could see this as me being quite defeatist by this; I'm not advocating that this is the position that people should take, I am merely pointing out that there is a reality to all this that does impact how time affects us.

I wanted to focus on these 2 areas to highlight what I consider to be the main aspects as to how time can be eroded away, through a combination of how we view it, and also how we have it stolen from us, especially where for whatever reason we are limited financially in being able to make more use from it. It might well be that I am stating the obvious, or this could be an example of me demonstrating overthinking in all its glory. Regardless of either of these facts, whether true or not, I'm putting it out there because for me it's a right pain in the fucking arse.

So, the question is 'what can you do about it? I have in part tried to offer some explanation as to the first aspect which I concluded that it was difficult to 'unthink' what you know because you are set in your ways as to your learning habits. Although it is difficult, it could be that there are ways to try and perhaps do a number of small things differently, as opposed to any major overhaul of your life that will be too challenging to fully commit to. The fact that I have referred to these is because it is not without efforts being made that I have tried to take these on, and somewhat experiment with them in an effort to see if there is anything that can be done to possibly make them more palatable.

With regards to the first part, as to reducing or refining your learning, the simple solution could be viewed as a reduction in what you are exposed to. This though is far from easy.

If, for example, you want to be less exposed to what I referred to as 'bollocks', it is here that I have purposely turned my attention in trying to focus only on what I consider to be worth 'knowing'. This in practice mostly consists of watching or reading up on copious amounts of news, which can in part be useful, in as much that there is an opportunity to take on knowledge that provides you with information that in turn allows you to get depressed, whilst also allowing you to be mainly sanctimonious to anyone who is also mainly sanctimonious. This provides for fantastic entertainment in allowing you to fall out with people who you both agree and disagree with and possibly ruining perfectly good friendships.

It is indeed possible through this process to 'learn' information that is collectively more relevant, it's not however necessarily more advantageous as to how this offers any real benefit. News can be not only be repetitive, it is also prone to providing you with 'bollocks', in the way of questionable newsworthiness material. [7]

So, certainly as a standalone method, I would argue that this is not really worth pursuing, as it merely gives you access to a world of ridiculous amounts of subjectivity and an increased push towards disliking people, even more than you currently already do.

The next option is to 'read up' on certain specific subjects that you might also deem as worth knowing, potentially being important enough to be worthy of sharing. As to providing any examples, this would firmly sit within the camp that perhaps may be demonstrable in being beneficial to the recipient in some way or the other.

In essence this would lean more towards what me might refer to as 'educational knowledge'. There is no real

---

7 see any last 5 minute news section

negative as to attempting this, however there are still a number of factors that do need to be considered. This could be firstly having a genuine interest in whatever you are studying, and secondly, and maybe more importantly, having the ability to learn or apply yourself in what you are studying. An example of how futile this might be, with regards to myself, would be me to learn about knitting. Firstly, I couldn't give a fuck about knitting, and secondly my fingers are too fat to be able to do any knitting.

You could (at a push), equally see both as a worthwhile challenge, however I would only consider this to be an even more wasteful use of time than learning about 'bollocks', I mean regardless of whether or not anybody else gives a shit, at the very least learning about 'bollocks' is something that you can do quite easily, mainly because there is a lot of it out there to consume.

Certainly though, it would be right to see this as the area of time spent that is more productive and healthier as a learning pursuit, providing that you can quickly determine whether or not you can indeed apply yourself in the right way.

It could well be that I am giving time too much credit and by placing so much emphasis on it, I could be giving it too much respect. Although I still consider myself to be young (in mind at least), I have become more aware of the passage of time and have started to begin to question my own mortality. I can only judge this through my own experiences, and for me, a lot has to be said about the effect that having children has. Both my kids are 11 and 14 and to see them now really brings home how quickly these years have gone. This is made worse as they are now as people (especially my teenage son), where they are living the part of their lives that is very much part of defining who they will eventually become, blissfully unaware of how this is unfolding. Additionally, what also brings this home when you see a lot of you in them; both in the sense that you want them to achieve more, and not fall victim to making any of the same mistakes that you made, knowing though that ultimately you are powerless to really have any say in this whatsoever.

I don't know whether or not there are equivalences to those that do not have children, it might be that they also consider their own mortality but for different reasons. All I do know is that for my own situation, this very much forms a huge part of my thinking.

I began this chapter talking about an obsession with time. I do think this remains very true to me, however instead of the attraction for wanting to see time pass, it has turned into a desire to slow it down. I'm probably less enthusiastic about the future, but this is not to say that I am not hopeful for my kids and their kids etc. It will be harder, but I think they are overall better at understanding the challenges and much more applied in dealing with the shit that older generations have both caused and ignored, either because they generally don't know better, or refuse to accept some of the realities as it inconveniences them either financially or presents a required change of lifestyle. We should be hopeful, it's the least we can fucking do.

As I write this, I suddenly become quietly distracted by a sense of guilt or anxiety as to whether admitting this somewhat makes me a bit odd, but equally I am aware that I am not only stating the fucking obvious, but I am projecting a lot of the same fears, concerns or questions that plenty of other people experience. Another part of me is fully aware of how 1st worldish this all sounds, moaning about the challenges of time in an environment where I am fortunate to be given so much more than other people. When I view it like this, I actually feel pretty twatish, you know in that way where when you say something out loud you realise that you are basically full of shit. That fucking way.

To try and stay on point and draw this to a conclusion though, I have chosen to focus on time, as to how this as an entity* impacts what we do.[8]

Given how we spend it, as exampled by how much shite I have written, despite this, I consider this as good evidence as to why being more ignorant may be better suited to how you experience time. With my new found respect for the 'bliss' element of it, the word 'ignorant' may be a bit harsh. In this context and allowing for the serenity that *'to be ignorantly bliss'* offers, it would be better to refer now to it as being *'optimistically vacant'*.

---

8 *could not think of a better word.

Please note that I would still love to have a time machine though and when NASA and the deep state governments of the world get exposed, I am looking forward to getting one from Argos.

Money

I'm not poor, I'm actually quite fucking far off it, however I am still burdened by how much money I do have at my disposal. I am fully aware as to the fine lines and being careful not to come across as a complete dick, so apologies in advance if whatever I write comes across as dickish. Context is going to be important here, so I'll do my best.

I've always had a strange relationship with money, which I am sure is from growing up where money was not something that I ever equated with good; mainly because there was either a lack of it, which often meant that when this happened (and it was a lot), but there was a level of inconvenience to it. Not just in the way of say having to go to your grannies to get fed, it was the inconvenience that it had on the wider perception of a family unit, not just from thoughts of other people, but your family as well. Even when it appeared that we had money, there was always some catch to it, whereby whatever immediate joy it offered in the way of purchasing all the must have items, (think 80's and 90's, VHS recorders, Big Yellow Teapots etc), this was very quickly undone when it came to how money had to work in actually paying for said items.

I'm not going to go into specific details, but as a summary from memory, it was mainly to do with either not ever actually having enough money and then not being able to manage it. There is a lot to be said about the traps that people are exposed to because of this; it's quite relentless in how unforgiving it is and how easy it is for it to become a vicious cycle which is incredibly hard to get out of.

It is stupid and unfair to suggest that this is only something that impacts people from poorer backgrounds, but there is a key difference that is significant, and it centres around the problems caused by both not having enough money and also not being able to manage it. This is all made messier because of the subjectivity of 'needs' and 'wants'.

One of the biggest misconceptions of poverty, or those on low incomes, is always that there is a quick judgement made against what the money they have (or don't have), is spent on. The narrative is that the reasons that this exist is because people are buying massive fucking 50-inch TV's, smoking and drinking and having takeaways. To have, or to do any of this almost demonised and it is the perfect excuse to castigate a group in a way that so that it is easier to give less of a shit about them. This is not a new mindset either.

Without going into the wider arguments of all of this, I just want to draw attention to it the fact that regardless of whether there is any truth as to certain views from a group of people, it is without doubt that it does begin a process, or an awareness that you are suddenly being judged. The less you have, the more you are judged because it positions or pigeonholes you, firmly intended that you might take notice and aspire to at a particular level in society.

The irony is that the judgement is often being made by those that not only 'have or do' all of the above, but they also 'have and do' more. It's not necessarily because they have done anything different in achieving this, it's often just because they have had access to more opportunities for one reason or another.

So, in the pursuit of daring to the wants of 'have or do', something we are conditioned to believe is almost a minimum socially accepted standard; this is based on this being decreed as acceptable, subject to a number of conditions being adhered. The quick 'go to' here, and undoubtedly the wider consensus is 'you can't afford it, so you can't have it'. So, on one hand you are judged to be somewhat inferior, or looked down upon if you don't have certain things that are socially expected of you to 'fit in'. You are then judged if you do have these things, yet then are judged again, when you have little or no money that has been used in part in purchasing these things? The scary thing is that we are all complicit in this, and there is nothing better than judging people is there? It works both ways too, it's upwards, downwards, sideways, it's all over the fucking place.

I don't intend to go all 'political' with this, the reason I want to make a point of it is that with reference to the theme of the book, it does, and has contributed to what I have done or not done through my life, although the anomaly is that it's not because of what I identified as to the constraints of limited finances. In my adult life I can't say that I haven't had enough money and neither have I had an inability to understand or manage money.

Whilst it is regrettably true that I have fallen victim to societal pressures to have many of the current required items of mandatory materialistic shite, I have by default arrived at a position which has resulted in me questioning other expenditure on things that sit outside this spectrum. It is both because of my experiences with money (or lack of it) growing up, combined with a self-awareness of what societal expectancy there is, this has formed the basis as to how I use money. This mainly consists of me assessing needs over wants, which on the face of it is fine, however it is because of my earlier experiences in life that I somehow have managed more often than not, to conclude that I don't actually want anything. It's not to the degree of being frugal or never buying stuff, however when it comes to 'pushing the boat out', it has always been really difficult to do this. For me, in order to be consistent, it was, and always has been important to take the view in determining that it was to be cooler to have less materialistic shite, and also my mission to find fault in those aspirational pursuits that require a lot of money to do, e.g. going on wanky cruises, playing golf, having a flash car etc.

I distinctly remember being a teenager and finding myself in this transitional stage that allowed for the opportune time to cement, or nurture a way of thinking that would go on to shape my decisions when tempted by any consumerism. I recall for a period of time being fixated on having a pair of Adidas Torsion trainers, as this, among other things was an item that was a golden ticket towards being seen as cool. Although having this boost, in reality, I knew early on that it was not something that I could be arsed to make the required effort to uphold. It wasn't actually about money either, not directly at least. For me, I think now as I did then, that people walking around constantly in tracksuits and trainers look a bit dickish. It's kind of okay if you happen to know that they are about to go, or recently finished some sporting-based activity, but to just wear one for the sake of it? I mean come on, what the fuck is all that about?

I think additionally I was fortunate for one reason or another for it not to be important, as I never felt that feeling that you have to display your wanky items to people to either show off or fit in, was just desperate. I mean, I took the view that if that is some sort of a key driver to gaining friends, it's all a bit weak or genuinely sad that someone feels that they have to do this.

It's not about necessarily singling this out because of the money associated with this either, but I concede perhaps subconsciously I was thinking this.

This experience was very influential though, it did start to make me think about what I thought I wanted and began to question whether or not this was important enough to demonstrate value, which we know is subjective depending on what the 'want' is.

Importantly though, and this is what I do believe plays a part in our relationship with money, that at the heart of it, a lot comes down to how able we are to weigh up not only the '*needs v wants*', but also weigh up the social aspects of it. There is a lot to be said by really not giving a flying fuck as to how people view what you do and do not have. If you can truly think this way, personally, I believe this to be one of the ingredients towards contentment. Whether it is possible to always have this attitude is another matter though.

As with how time binds us with responsibilities, our perspective of money is not necessarily left to our own choices though on what we are prepared to spend it on. Not just on the shit that we have to either e.g. bills etc, but also through our social situation or circumstances, whether we are in a relationship, married with or without kids, or even on our own, we find ourselves buying shit because we either believe we have to, or are pressured to as a prerequisite of fitting in. Nobody is really held under duress here; it is a case that we convince ourselves that for some reason this will make a difference for good in our lives or the lives of others. If we are honest, I think the problem is that whilst this can indeed be the case, there still remains a lot to be said as to the fact that we know a lot of this is bullshit. It helps to reduce buyer's remorse though, so that's good.

Given what I have said, I am aware my views on this is overtly negative and I know that I am viewing this through the prism of my own bias. It is true that through money there is a lot to be said as to what differences that it can make to your quality of life, and anyone who would lay claim to not having more of it is lying. Having access to an abundance of money is likely to bring you closer to greater freedoms through the ability to do more of those things that we believe will make us happier, whether it be going on extravagant holidays, driving nice cars or eating out at posh restaurants. This is simply because it removes or reduces the pressures of our responsibilities. Really though, when you strip it down to it's simplest form, the fact remains that we are heavily influenced by what we are told will make us happy, and a lot of this is linked to the perception that others may have of us when we are seen to be spending money on certain things. It is this that makes me resentful over money, it's not necessarily about the reality that there will be vast differences as to the amount of money that people have, (even though this is wrong as well), it's more to do with how we have let consumerism set these benchmarks for us all, based on the money that we have, which in turn creates this downward snobbery and upward jealousy. To me, I just see it as not only a waste of time but also a load of bollocks.

It is because of this that I have found myself almost deliberately trying to expose this fallacy through convincing myself, or refusing to participate in falling victim to spending money on those things that are a ‘must have’. Again, this is not because I can’t do this, it is because I have no desire to conform to it, as similar to my experience with the trainers, I know that it won’t necessarily make me happy. Sure, it might make me more sociably accepted by a certain group of people, but if you determine that this is what you have to do to be happy, I think this is quite a deluded position to take. If you need an example of this, consider all those people that you know who have constantly made it their mission to boast about how much money they have, but also then brag about all the wanky things they do. Whether or not they are happy is something that arguably only they will know. Whether or not everyone thinks they are cunts, is pretty much guaranteed.

The fact is though that I do know this has impacted me negatively at times. It is through these assertions that I have become something of a ‘reverse snob’, which has meant that I have through my own stubbornness, elected not to have spent money on things that in the most likelihood would have actually made me happy. Deep down though, I am aware enough to know that the reason I am this way is predominantly due to the fact that I have a fear of money because of my early experiences with it. I don’t believe this to be wholly bad, but I can recall plenty of times where it has influenced my decisions and I have missed out.

What I would say is that as I have got older, I have found that I have a slightly different perspective, which is what I consider to be a balanced 'fuck it' approach to spending. I'm better now at not feeling compelled to overanalyse the things that I spend my money on, and a lot of this is because I have been keen to give my kids access to more of the things that they have decided will make them happy, but also because of an increased sense of my own mortality and the fact that because I might die within the next 50 years, this somehow offers greater justification towards spending money on shit that I don't need. I'm not necessarily extravagant, but I have definitely started to be a lot less cautious, for example, I will regularly go into Poundland quite willing about to fill the entire basket with loads of random items, smug in the knowledge that by the time I reach the till, not only can I afford it, but I could easily go round the shop again several times repeating this feat.

The subject of money could be seen as an easy target, something that you can blame for any ills that you have, or drawing attention to how it has caused you to miss out on the things in life that are so readily available to others. In many ways though, this is not only not true, but also a sure-fire way to easily become disenfranchised with the things that you have, consumed by forever wanting more.

I think in truth that it's okay to want more, but the mistake that is often made is that we equate this with what we spend our money on, or the idea that this is the only way that we can accomplish this. The reality is that we don't have to aspire to have those things that are financially outside our reach to be happy. We don't have to be envious of those things that others have that we do not, and neither should we look down on those less fortunate than ourselves.

I don't know whether or not I will change my views on this further as I get older and possibly more fancy free with how I spend my money. Maybe there is an inevitability that at some point in time you will find yourself driving a sports car, going on some wanky cruise or indeed playing fucking golf. Maybe we don't have any choice in this, maybe our brains are hardwired so that we see this as a requirement of getting to a certain age or in line with whatever social demographic we happen to find ourselves in. Until such time though, I like to think that I will continue to fight the good fight, slandering John Lewis and other similar establishments, whilst helping to financially contribute towards Poundlands ever growing global dominance.

It's not a drug, it's a drink

This will be fun.

I'm not against alcohol but I am against me drinking alcohol, or certain people drinking alcohol.[9] This is not intended to sound preachy and you could easily substitute the words 'drinking alcohol' for 'eating polo mints'. For some people, polo mints can turn them into a right twat.

9 As of this precise moment in time

I think our relationship with alcohol is strange in as much that it revolves around both an acceptance of some of the problems that can occur through drinking, yet at the same time, generally it's seen as an okay thing to do because it is worth the fun that it brings.

I wouldn't disagree with the latter part of this as clearly it is something that most people can drink without any real impact on their lives. They can function perfectly fine and if anything, it offers a nice relief to whatever stresses or strains that they might be dealing with. The thing that I find interesting about alcohol though is trying to understand the journey that people go with this, and how certain personality types react when on it. For me, it's an easier conversation to have now, mainly because I can be more honest about how it affects me, and as it currently stands, I am now a nondrinker[10]. This is not because I am an alcoholic though, it is mainly because I simply cannot deal with hangovers anymore.

As to exploring this further, it's worth thinking about how we either reach this type of decision, or how we relate with it.

My first dalliance with alcohol was when I was around 12 years old. Apart from the odd sneaky sip of my Dad's Hoffmeister or drinking Shandy Bass, there was nothing before then. This is not to say I wasn't exposed to other people on alcohol though.

---

10 As of this precise moment in time

I remember pretty accurately that this came about through me, my friends who were 13 and 16, having a sleepover, watching wrestling, Neighbours in German (which we dubbed over), accompanied by all the usual teenage treats but additionally 2 x 2ltr bottles of Strongbow. At about 2am, we had a wrestling match, someone got an undefrosted gateau thrown their face, and we woke up at 7.

That's all I can remember from the later part of the shenanigans, apart from the next day. The next day I felt fine.

I didn't drink again until I was around 15, and then as with most teenagers it became the thing to do. The taboo aspect made it infinitely more enticing and in the pursuit of acquiring this, made it what is was. And just like that, it became as a week-to-week event (mainly Fridays), as common as going to school. For me personally, the only thing that changed after 18, was not necessarily any increased frequency to drinking, it was just an easier item to get your hands on.

I imagine that most people will recall similar experiences with alcohol through youth to young adulthood, and I would imagine that by and large, most of this was mixed with the number of amplified angsts of youth and other various aged related generalisations. The important difference though was that there was also an abundance of lack of hangovers. I think this is arguably one of the key factors as to how we view alcohol. Some of us associate it with fun and all that happy shit, which I think is precisely because of our ability to not fall victim to the hangover. The other factor though is the contributory elements of our alcoholic exploits that go into making you feel like utter wank the next day.

It is here though that I would like to draw attention to the affects that personality traits have and the reasons why.

First and foremost, I believe that a certain amount of consideration must go in our prior experiences of alcohol that we witnessed through whatever social environment that we found ourselves in. In many ways, this, coupled with whatever other exposures we had (film, tv etc), meant that we formulated, or proselytised as to how we might conduct ourselves when drinking. In many ways, this is no different from how we might conduct ourselves in any situation, however the key component of control is diminished (or in extreme cases removed), as we become inebriated.

So, what we essentially end up with is a mishmash of who we are, who we think we should be, who we might want to be, and who we don't want to be. It's a lovely eclectic mix.

There are levels, but in essence, the way that we act, especially when we first start drinking begins to contribute to how we then lead our lives. This is both in terms of the social aspects, or should I say invitational gatherings, but also the consequential after events. This is not to say that this is necessarily a negatively disruptive force, but it does mean that depending on the type of person that you are, it can result in shaping thoughts or actions because of this.

We will do this whether our experiences were good or bad, however, regardless of either, what also appears to happen is that people form opinions of others based on this. As to how influential this is, ultimately depends on how you are affected by it and why? It might be that you don't give a fuck, it could be that it galvanizes you, or it could be that it makes you feel bad. To say that it doesn't add to a perception of an individual though is not true. It's worth noting that this is also applicable for people who don't drink as well. [11]

Any behaviours though are down to how we perceive these views ourselves and this can influence who we become. For me, the challenges I have had with alcohol has very much been based on feeling compelled to join in, being unable to handle my drink, and lastly, and most importantly and indeed further perplexing, is my actual dislike of the taste of it. Again, these are all components that I am sure many will relate to, but I would consider that when you add a persons mood, this will nurture the perfect environment for a particular type of 'drunk', to emerge. They've already got their various labels, its just a question of which you fall into the most. Let's have a look at what we are dealing with:

1) The happy drunk

This will typically be someone who spends a vast portion of the night, laughing (not aggressively mind), who

---

11 Never trust a man who doesn't drink. What is that all about?

generally appear to be having a nice time and not being offensive. They will occasionally slur their words, and be a little bit sleepy. All in all, their contribution is memorable for people who will recall them as 'lovely'.

2) The funny drunk

This is subjective based on your interpretation of funny. It could well be that we might accept that within a close-knit group of friends they are seen as funny. In a closed environment, such as sitting in someone's house, the outcome or end result is quite clear. Everyone will probably me more relaxed and it's all cool. When you explore this further though, it gets a little more convoluted by virtue of the fact that funny then gets measured across how it received by others, so in a pub type environment, depending on the distance the 'comedy' travels, the differences can be significant. There can be a tendency for funny to be offensive and this can be problematic, especially when it results in literal fighting because of it.

Overall, though, this type of drunk, if remembered as funny, is generally seen as an important ingredient to how well the evening was. Additional consideration though. Everyone thinks they are funny when they are drunk, drunk funny can be confrontational and drunk funny can also be dangerous. If you sit with a group of friends who are drinking through the night, and you are sober, what is considered as funny becomes a lot less subjective. Try it.

3) Emotional drunk

It's a bit unfair to go to hard on the emotional drunk. Their motive for drinking is basically medicinal. This type of drunk will normally siphon off individuals within a group of friends when something really shit has happened, e.g. break-up. At first, they seek out a confidant, who they will see as crucial to sharing their pain with. At some point, because confidant becomes unavailable/disinterested (delete accordingly), they will seek out others in the hope that they may offer invariably a repeat of the advice that you have already received from confidant, but on a bigger scale. If through the passage of time, the emotional drunk has not managed to rectify whatever shit made them feel down, any sympathy goes out the fucking window, advice becomes more aggressive, and some potential alienation may occur.

It is a pure lottery as to whether any success can happen when consuming alcohol in this mindset. Social drinking is more likely to achieve success, as in a way out, as solo drinking just renders a further spiral of decline in which it could result in you listening to Sarah McLachlan or Damien Rice albums.

4) Angry drunk

WATCH OUT, (think WWE commentator), the angry drunk is here. This person will be furious from the outset, in fact for at least the first hour, they will lay down the foundations with full details as to why they are so furious. The objective is often to seek either permanent or temporary removal of such frustration through consumption of alcohol.

What often happens, is that for a short period of time, any anger appears to be tempered. Unfortunately, though, if too much time elapses, frustrations creep back and full anger resumes. This is very much similar in part to funny, as to how it travels, as to the subsequent consequences. Mainly, this comprises of various friends telling angry person to calm down and apologising to various individuals or groups of people. Regarded as annoying and definitely a downer on the night.

5) Sexytime drunk

This person is on a mission. Whilst they might not necessarily be covert in their operation, largely due to them stating from the outset as to their intentions, their night means they become quite nomadic.

As company goes, they are quite vacant and it is difficult to talk about anything other than their pursuits. Where night draws in, this can go a number of ways which may or may not have resulted in original mission plans. Can become ridiculously obvious and can result in friends once again apologising to individuals or groups. Definitely, prone to much piss taking based on outcome.

6) Sober drunk

If anyone never wanted to be somewhere it is this person. Their appearance or demeanour is one that might be construed as dismissive. They will be drinking, although there is clearly a reluctance in doing so and they will mainly informing everyone that everything is shit. Not quite argumentative but certainly confrontational enough to be annoying. They will have limited interaction outside their own group and will either leave early or see it through to the bitter end and then just magically disappear.

7) The ‘I know it all’ drunk

Whatever anyone has done, this person has done it at least twice and will insist that they have done it better. This on its own is okay, based on the fact that others will start to pick up on this and the ‘I know it all’ drunk will soon be the one that people are ripping the piss out of when they leave the table. The danger is how deep conversations go as to the true extent of damage that this person can cause. Politics, Religion and Love Island are topics that should be avoided at all costs.

8) The ‘I’m not drunk’ drunk

It is without doubt that this person will definitely be drunk way before anybody else is, and it is at this point where their night solely becomes all about them insisting that they are not drunk, often demonstrated by a fantastic inability to grasp the English language by slurring or mispronouncing every other word. Unfortunately, this is a race that they simply cannot win and will forever be slightly ahead with how inebriated they are. Depending on how the night pans out, their moment in the spotlight will either mean that they fall asleep, at which time it is possible for them to become a version of Bernie, from 'Weekend at Bernies', used as some sort of prop to entertain people, or they just kind of flop around, popping up randomly at other peoples tables. It is here, they make efforts to redeem themselves by insisting once again that they are not drunk, only to be exposed early on by the shit that comes out of their mouths. This person is harmless and, in many ways, the romanticised version of what we think being drunk should be.

9) The 'I'm fucking really really drunk' drunk

Your mission, should you accept it, is to get absolutely trashed as quickly as possible. As to why this is their goal, it could be for a myriad of reasons. This person will basically combust after a short period of time, before they either fall asleep, wet themselves or injure themselves etc. Despite any of these occurring, they will somehow come to life (albeit in a zombie state), and will be seen propped up against a wall eating a kebab and the wrapper.

The impact on friends is that it will result in one good Samaritan stopping their own drinking to become a carer for the night. The following days will see this person reflect deeply on their adventures, at least for 2 days before they are back on it again the following weekend.

I am sure that there are others that I have missed, or certainly aspects in each category that could be further elaborated on. I have tried to cover those that I would consider to be the ones that resonate with most people. That, or I have just projected the states I have got myself in.

Crucially though, given these various types of drunks that people become, as to the ramifications, it is a case of looking at the frequency of the type of drunk that a person is that offers a real insight as to who the person is when they don't drink. People often cite that alcohol loosens or reflects a persons true behaviours or thoughts, and whilst there may be some truth to this, I think really this is largely inaccurate and potentially damaging from a psychological position. It's too simplistic to view the actions of someone who is drunk as a reflection of their personality or current situation. Sometimes, it can simply be a case that someone can't handle their drink and it can result in them simply being a dick. Sure, if it is something that happens as a regular occurrence, then yes, maybe it can be attributed to an underlying issue, but to go to this position straight away can be unfair and actually create a problem that perhaps wasn't there.

Whatever your experiences or views may or may not be as to any of these stereotypes, they are all in one way or another symptomatic as to not only contributing to our character, but yet another factor in possibly preventing us from doing certain things in our lives. Again, this takes us back towards the whole *'ignorance is bliss'* arena, where it can be the case that some people might look at these through a certain philosophical lens, which is really just that they deem all of this to be a condition, or a reality of what happens when people drink. I think that there is a lot of truth to this, especially when what is often discounted is that when everyone is drinking, everyone is having their own unique experience, which dilutes your concerns as to what others might think of you. Not all the time, but certainly more than we think.

I knew when deciding to write about this that there was a requirement for a degree of honesty, which I am quite chilled out about, especially now being someone who has chosen not to drink. I still maintain though that my new found resistance to alcohol has been the insufferable hangovers that now go on forever. Personally speaking, it is this coupled then with the overthinking that in combination often feels like I am in hell. I know that sounds a bit extreme, but it is the truth, in as much that it is what I might equate hell to being like.

I do think there is a slight societal change going on with alcohol though, not to the extent where people are no longer getting pissed and getting up to whatever pissed people do, but it is much more common place to see individuals electing to drink less, or not at all, without necessarily feeling like a social pariah. It could well be that I'm being slightly naïve thinking this, as a counterpart to this (if Facebook is to be believed), is that everyone is appears to be wanting to get pissed. It might be that I have just stumbled into my own social group where there is less of an emphasis on drinking, or it could be that it's one of the realities of getting older and questioning your efforts towards healthy living.

If there was anything that I have been most susceptible to, with regards to feeling a certain obligation to do, up until about 10 years ago, was to join in with various alcohol themed activities. It is without doubt that though that with hindsight this by and large was always a mistake, mainly because the reality for me as an individual was that I am more prone to the negative aspects that alcohol offers. Despite this though, I think because of the social pressures to 'join in', this was somewhat enough to override any concerns or self-awareness that I probably should avoid at all costs. I think when you are younger, this is a reality that a lot of people face. It's that balance of weighing up what we are made to believe that of what we should be doing in the way of drinking, (for what really is a short period of time in our week), against that of the effects that doing this has on us (for the longer period of time in our week/lives). It's probably the epitome of pleasure and pain, and for some, including me, it is the pain part that seems to resonate more, especially in recent years.

As I have said though, it is not fair to attribute my experiences with alcohol to be a universal norm, far from it. If anything, on the face of it, this is an infliction that appears to only be experienced by the minority.

Quite possibly, it might be something that people are afraid to admit to. It could well be that any vexations that people have are ignored because they are unable to either be self-aware of any problems that they may be having as a direct result of drinking, or indeed they might not feel that they are able to make any changes to the way it affects them. It could be though that I am simply talking a load of bollocks and trying to make excuses for past ventures.

I don't begrudge anyone who drinks, and if indeed it is something that a person likes to do, enjoys the experience, and believe it has no negative, or limited impact on their lives, then no problem. It's not because I now have made the decision not to drink that I intend to come across as sanctimonious. All I can say is that as to the difference that this has brought to me is that I have begun to notice that I am able to do more. It does mean that there is a level of sacrifice as to knowingly making a decision to refrain from partaking in certain social activities, although this is a sacrifice that is ultimately better for everyone.

It could well be that arriving at this realisation is because I am now a bit older and a bit wiser that this is an easier position to take. It is definitely true that to adopt this mindset has been hugely helped because of the hangovers, but for now, it appears that it has been the right corrective action to take.

In an ideal world, it may have been a decision that I took earlier, especially given how much more shit I appear to be able to do, alongside a greater feeling of tranquillity and being at peace with myself.

Just to conclude though, and this is applicable to pretty much anyone who drinks on a regular basis, here is some math that I think is worth considering.

1 night drinking = 1 day hangover
52 nights drinking = 52 days of hangover (per year)
25 years drinking x 52 days of hangover = 1300 days

That's nearly 4 years of your life sat on a couch, with a headache, eating shit loads of food, and doing fuck all.

I accept that it is easy to equate various things that we do as a method of questioning the validity or justification of this (often mostly used by people who don't smoke). Maybe it's something that we need to do so that it gives us some perspective as to whether indeed we deem it to be a worthwhile activity that we wish to continue to do.

If you didn't know this mathematical equation, you fucking do now.

Work

I appear to find myself writing this chapter at the same time as I have returned to work. Although I did have this down as a topic that I wanted to discuss, the fact that I am writing about this now is purely down to coincidence as opposed to by design. That said it is quite apt, as even though it has only been a few days since I have returned, I am currently in that state of mind which is dominated by those holiday thoughts, where prior to your return you made a number of commitments to yourself with the intent to implement changes that you hope will bring greater harmony and joy in whatever role you do.

There is a lot to be said as to where you currently are in the job spectrum (loving your job to absolutely despising it), as to what these proposed changes are likely to be. I will come back to this later though.

All of what I say here is probably going to be quite contentious, as although there will always be things about the world of work that people can agree on, there are so many variables at play surrounding our own individual experiences. Therefore, more than ever, and in line with my other attempted virtuous disclaimers I have made in earlier chapters, I feel that before I start to go off on some diatribe about the world of work, I am again very much aware that this will come across as wanky and self-absorbed. It could, or almost certainly will sound like I have overthought this, and finally any bitching I do is superfluous, especially in comparison to some of the jobs that people have to do both here in the UK, as well as in other countries. I don't imagine for example that anything that I have experienced will ever be on par with wading through mountains of rubbish to find plastic, or clearing a sewer of fatbergs. And neither is it intended to sound like I am making fun of the people that have to do these jobs.

Hopefully, despite the obvious stark differences in the jobs that I have done, there will be some universal truths that I am able to refer to[12]. If not, then I've been doing the whole work thing wrong for a long fucking time.

Given the significance that work has on our lives (outside of family and friends), in so many ways it forms the basis, or foundations for all that we may want to do. It is for this reason that there is a lot to be said as to why we are conditioned from a young age to understand why it is important to give ourselves the best opportunities by working hard at school, to not only find a job or a career that will offer us the financial rewards incumbent with living a particular desired lifestyle, but additionally we are also told (or at least it is inferred), that we will benefit from having an occupation that we will enjoy doing. [13]

Whilst I fundamentally agree with the above sentiment, the issue that I mainly have, is that I am convinced that a lot of this is complete and utter bollocks.

My reasoning for this is that unbeknown to us when we are given these early instructions, in the background, what we are not necessarily made aware of, is the levels of social engineering that runs parallel to us beginning at the start of this journey. This should not be confused with what we already know as to the higher levels of elitism that has, (and always will) exist within our society; this is more of a 'micro' version, where from the outset, despite the

12 Mainly wanky office jobs
13 Societies happiness equation

unknowns with regards to a young person's abilities, decisions and judgements are being made of them. This will be done by those either charged with not just the responsibility to educate, but others who are in a position to exert some influence, such as parents of other children etc.[14] This is to an extent similar to the same factors that relate to the judgement made towards people based on the perceived amount of wealth they might have, although it is here where if anything, this actually contributes towards where an individual ends up. This is a sort of mapping out, or a 'you better know your place' instruction, that sets the tone for the formative years.

The reason that I wanted to draw on this was because I do think that it is something that can easily be dismissed, especially by the time that we enter the world of work, as it is far easier to revert to the classic rhetoric of someone simply not working hard enough as to the main, or only reason as to why a person is not in a 'good job' or a job that they want to do.[15] What are the determining factors?

I'm all for people working harder to achieve more and I fully accept that for some people, there is a reality that they will have to work harder to achieve that which comes easier to others. Equally, I'm also aware that there are individuals, who despite those extra hurdles, have gone on to achieve their goals. In reality this is the exception though, whatever fucking spin anyone wants to put on it.

---

14 Especially parents who are on the PTA

15 Define 'good job'

What do we mean when we use the term ‘work harder’? Has anyone ever said to you that you must work harder when you have been busting your balls? It can be subjective as fuck, especially if it’s said by an autocrat.

As to the relevance, I think there are a lot of inequalities and this leads to a shit load of people falling into jobs that they would have never really wanted to do. And if they are not currently in this job that they never really wanted to do, through lack of opportunities, they are now actively seeking out a job that they never really wanted to do. Sure, people will manufacture some sort of narrative when talking to others that it is indeed the job that they always wanted to do, but in secret, they won’t really.

Of course, there is an argument to be had where a person will not necessarily know what career they wish to embark on, and it is also true that it is possible that a person can find themselves in a position where suddenly they are naturally suited and can go on to excel further. This happens to a lot of people, especially for those that manage to find themselves fortunate to work for a company that values them, which goes a long way towards a person believing that they are truly in a job that they want to be doing.

Whatever way you look at it though, this all comes down to a level of internal compromising that people do, in order that they can feel better about whatever it is they are doing. Yes, people can indeed work hard and end up in a job they always wanted to do, but I would bet good money that this is quite a small minority. How many people that you know, if asked to provide an honest answer as to whether they were in a job that not only they are happy in, but also it is the job that they always wanted to do?

With my own experiences of work and the various jobs that I have had, I am always surprised when speaking to people, who, when you eventually find out more about them, discover that what they originally set out to do can be a million miles away from what they actually doing now. I've seen this both with people who are in different jobs to me, and with people doing exactly the same job as me. It is this that I have to admit has left me at times wondering what the point has been in following a certain path, if at the end of it, I would have ended up in exactly the same place without the need to have followed a set of instructions that I was led to believe would put me at an advantage.

For me, this just reaffirms the notion that for many of us, the process that we go through in the pursuit of the career or job that we want to do, feels a bit pointless. Meanwhile, as this reality sets in, you find yourself surrounded by people who are clearly doing jobs that they can't do, and they are often paid handsomely for it.

I do concede that it is important to acknowledge that there is a lot to be said as to how we see ourselves, often convinced that we are better than we really are, but at the same time it doesn't detract that we can experience various forms of criticism when we believe that it might not be warranted. Depending on our own sense of value, the higher this is, the more of a negative impact it can have as to how we deal with it. Additionally, who we are as people with regards to our traits or personalities will affect how we deal with this. When you also consider the relationship between you and the deliverer of the criticism, this also can have a profound effect.

There is a lot I have written here, as some sort of preamble (or at least that's how it seems), because I think that it is too easy to just focus on some of the obvious aspects of our working lives as opposed to delving deeper to consider the roads taken. For me, possibly because it is easier to fully appreciate this now being in my forties and through experience, that by trying to look at work from a different perspective, I am now in a position that allows me to reduce my own frustrations with it. It's not that I am unable to accept that I have at times not performed in various roles that I have had; on balance my work ethic has actually been pretty good. I have busted my arse and been rewarded, I have busted my arse and not, and by and large experienced the usual high and lows that come with any jobs that we do.

Crucially though, there comes a point where there is a greater sense of your own identity and more of a focus on establishing a healthier work life balance that allows you to tick more boxes. I think it is because of this and an acceptance of not necessarily my own limitations, but certainly effort that I am prepared to put in towards those things at work that will either get noticed, or really make a difference. It is possible to be good at your job without fucking about with the politics of it. It's such a bizarre concept, when you are employed to do a specific job, e.g. data entry, completely unaware that suddenly you have to do this for a boss who dislikes spending money on equipment, which means you can't use the right software you need, a supervisor who constantly makes jokes about women, and then you are told to not speak to this or that person because they will throw you under a bus etc etc fucking etc.[16]

The more you comply, or assimilate to the environment, the more you let it impact your life. And the worse thing about this is that in the grand scheme of things, nobody gives a fuck. I'm not talking about the friendships that you can make, or even the things that you enjoy, this is mainly with reference to how much extra that you give towards your job that mostly goes unnoticed.

As of now, my philosophy is very much on being more relaxed about work. I'm less intent on trying to do more than I have to do because I don't really think it is worth it. Don't get me wrong, I'll gladly still continue to help others and do as I'm told, but no more or less than that. I guess this is my first real effort towards forcing myself to be more ignorant towards something in the hope that it means

16 Completely fictional scenario

I am more content. I think this is okay, and I do think people already do this. The issue is when we say it out loud we are conditioned that it is not and this is because there is a suggestion that we are lazy, ungrateful or disrespectful to your employer. It's really not though, if anything it's just not being prepared to play the game.

I originally had this idea that I would come at this making lots of references or various anecdotes about the jobs that I have had as I figured that this would offer me ample material which is extremely useful for when you are writing a book. Rather than do this though, I have chosen to talk about how we arrive where we do. It is this that is more revealing or useful, especially given that the theme of this book is about how certain things have a hold on us, or prevent us from pursuing activities etc. In our working lives, unlike the tongue and cheek mathematical equation previously used to highlight the wasted years lost through being hungover, when something similar is applied to the hours that we spend at work, it actually should be taken more seriously.

The reason it should is because as a percentage of time, week to week, year to year etc, this is where we are for the majority of our time. It is therefore something that warrants a lot of focus because it is important that we can try to get it as close to 'right' for us as possible. Again, this is my own personal view and my experiences would suggest that where we don't manage to do this, it only contributes towards a feeling of apathy towards doing certain things. The more unhappy that we are with anything that life throws at us, it is only natural that this demotivates us. By virtue of the fact then that we spend most of our time here, the significance that it has on how motivational or demotivational it is for us, means we should demand more from it. It is a fallacy though, or a mistake that we make though if we think that we are ever truly in control of how much influence that we can have in making this a reality. We certainly can't discount how much luck plays its part, and we never ever have control over this.

It could be that when reading this, you are either going to agree with some of what I have said, or conversely think I'm not only spouting a lot of shite, but also likely to call into question my work ethic. And as I said earlier, that's the natural response.

For anyone who might be just starting their careers, I wouldn't discourage anybody from going through the motions of doing those things that are necessary to develop or give yourself the opportunity to progress. Undoubtedly, if you don't at least go above and beyond, you will definitely reduce your chances of reaching your potential. All I would say is that it is important to identify when you are not achieving what you set out to do or not being recognised for what you do.

Lots of people can overstay their time in a job which unfortunately can be because they recognise the financial security that it provides them, putting this ahead of how it might actually make them feel. For some, they will be limited as to what they can really do about it.

We should be prepared to accept that when it comes to work and when we look for making a change, we do need to assess the risks associated should we decide to leave and venture towards something new. If it goes wrong, and this is something I have experienced, it can be difficult to deal with. You have effectively substituted something that you felt that wasn't right for you, possibly because of feeling underappreciated, to only then get told to fuck off by someone who really underappreciates you. It's fine lines that we are dealing with.

So, in coming back to the point I made at the beginning thinking about your current state on the love/hate your job spectrum, this should dictate a lot as to what you might do next. It is funny that this always seems to be more poignant or though of when we have been on holiday, although it shouldn't be that it takes a period of time to reflect on what is, or is not going right for us. The challenge is to identify it as quickly as possible and then look to do something about it. I think if we aren't proactive or assertive in trying to make things better, we not only lose the ability to be pragmatic, but when we do go back to work after a holiday, we will be much more inclined to return in full pissed off bastard mode.

Anyway, I think this will do on this chapter. This has by far been the most difficult thing to write about as unless you are talking about the generic work-based themes, you are only really offering thoughts on your own experiences of work. Our personal relationship with work doesn't mean that the chances of shared experiences won't exist; in many ways this allows us to feel that it's not just us. What we should be doing is possibly trying to understand why?

Health

This is the first time that I have written in just over 4 months. The main reason for this was two-fold, firstly because I was returning to work, and secondly because I had committed to running a half marathon. I had readily accepted that this would be a likely outcome, and despite my concerted and focused efforts towards my writing, I was actually okay about stopping for a bit. It could be that it might be construed that this is somewhat a lazy excuse, however the reality is that I am more self-aware of striking the right balance between my mental and physical capabilities. This is not to say that I am unable to push myself, but equally, I am much more comfortable just pausing to stop and take a step back if I need to.

For me, there is a lot to be said about how we can get this part of our lives right, and at the center of it is making a concerted attempt to not only acknowledge the importance of it, but to actually do something in addressing it.

Our relationship with health is strange if you consider that there are so many factors at play which ultimately contributes to how we believe that we can deal with it. This is further compounded by our attitude to how we view it. For some, it can be that some life changing event (possibly a near death experience), which then dictates some sort of mandatory response, trying to undo whatever damage has been done, whilst for others they may either feel nothing but contempt for it due to either a belief that they are actually immortal, or conversely, they accept that they are merely mortal and simply couldn't give a fuck. In any event, regardless to what a persons view is on health, whether this is mental, physical or both, fundamentally we are increasingly subjected to messages that we really should take notice of it and sort ourselves out.

There is nothing inherently wrong about this, especially given that we are all now living longer than at any other time in human history, but the payoff is that our fortuitous position that we find ourselves in comes with a price. The price being that if you truly want the opportunity to have greater longevity, you had better be prepared to work for it. If you don't, then the alternative is that you might still get there but you'll spend a shit load of time in various states of agony and pain in the process. Perversely, the irony is that should you elect to do something about it, you are also likely to endure pain and agony. The latter type just allows you to feel smug whilst you endure it.

My own relationship with health has been mixed.

One of the advantages that I had at a young age was that through the genetic soup that made me, I had the good fortune to be physically active and thin. By this I mean, when it came to running around, being sporty and basically action orientated, this just came natural to me. When plugged into the magic of youthful metabolism, I felt pretty much invincible. This invincibility however started to become much harder to maintain once I hit 16 and suddenly through a combination of puberty, alcohol, cigarettes, junk food and girls, my ability to sustain an appearance that I was content with suddenly became harder to maintain. If anything, though, and certainly I am viewing this with the benefit of hindsight, my experiences at this time are arguably reflective of what happens to lots of people. I was effectively 'off the market', extremely content with my environment, so there was no impetus or reason to be concerned over this sudden change to physically who I was. Sure, it was annoying as fuck being sometimes made ridicule as I had gained a belly or an extra chin, however in the grand scheme of things, mentally I was okay and even despite this increase of mass, I was still able to be active and more importantly retained a level of self-belief and determination to pretty much be able to continue to do whatever I had done before.

I am confident that my own experience is something that is quite common to young guys as the move through the teenage years towards becoming a man. There is no uniqueness to this and although there are variables as to how people make this step; the fact is that this is the beginning of a process where everything and anything that we physically do becomes more challenging. Proof of this is the reaction we have when we either sit down, or stand up. The older we get, the more this becomes both immensely pleasurable and equally painful at the same time. Our vocalisation and exaggeration of the words 'oooh' and 'argh' can be submitted as evidence. The former for sitting down, and the latter for standing up.

Crucially though, no matter who we are (or were), what we are not necessarily able to deal with or at least are prepared to deal with, is the increased pressures placed upon our mental health. In many ways, our physical indifferences is fairly straightforward, in as much that on the face of it, our new limitations in this area can to a certain extent be understood. We can be fairly philosophical as to whatever constraints we have because we readily accept that physically we are different because we have aged. Sure, there is a degree as to how far we might have declined because of this, however there is an acceptance or justification of this, which most of us can find a degree of humour in. This in itself is actually fine.

The problem is nothing to do with our physical limitations through simply getting old, the problem is how we are mentally afflicted. This is something that is not so easy to reconcile or indeed find humour in. What compounds this though is that the mental challenges that we face directly affects who we are physically. Not just in what we can physically do, but our physical representation that we wish to display.

Our mental health can be attributed to the circumstances that we find ourselves in, some because of the choices that we make and some that are thrust upon us.

Mostly though, it is my belief that is mainly external factors that force us to be reactive with the decisions that we make, all of which we are then forced to then internally deal with the consequences of whatever decision we arrived at. And so it continues, like some bizarre sort of game where we tell, or convince ourselves that we have control, and whilst there is some truth to this, it is foolish to believe that we truly are keepers of our own destiny. Our ability to stay mentally healthy is complicated because unlike the control that we have over our physical pursuits, our mental state is largely contingent on other people. It is therefore my assertion that Sartre was completely correct in his determination that 'hell is indeed other people'. Other people as to the impact on our minds, are mostly complete bastards, even if they don't necessarily intend to be.

When it comes to health, there is a great deal of 'chicken or the egg' going on, in as much that both our physical and mental health are intrinsically linked in a way where they contribute to how well we fair on both fronts. If we are physically active, there is a correlation as to how this affects us mentally by way of increased endorphins etc. Additionally, though, the more physically active we are, it does change our appearance in a way where we become more confident, which is reflected in not only the clothes we can now finally fit into, but our whole demeanour and the way that we interact is notably much more positive because we have an increased level of self-belief in who we are.

Whilst this is true, the issue here is the reason that we have probably achieved an improvement to our physical health is often due to a mental crash or realisation that we have felt compelled to make this change. So, on face value, although it is clear that we can boost our mental health through physical activity, it is only through the acceptance of, or a feeling of being low that we can begin to assert that we need to make changes in the first place, which begins with physical activity. What then happens is complacency.

The moment we start becoming 'healthy' in terms of being more active which makes us feel mentally more 'at one', we then more often than not reach a point where we know that to maintain this, it's basically a pain the arse. It's not necessarily a complete halt to this new life you have been crafting for yourself, it's much more of a slow decline towards reverting back to being what genuinely makes you feel content. The consideration here though which is often overlooked, is that what we consider to be content changes over time. Being content at 40, is a lot fucking different from being content at 20.

And this is the conundrum. On one hand we readily accept that the more sedentary that we are equates to a higher risk of becoming unhealthy, so we have to challenge ourselves mentally to then be become more physically active, which will boost us mentally, which, due to the ongoing efforts to be physically active becomes challenging, which then causes us to struggle mentally. So we then become less physical and then get mentally low because of this feeling of failure. And the older we are, the more difficult it automatically becomes to be more physically active. Either way, it's a right frigging hassle.

It is possible that I might just be referring to just my own experiences, however the fact of the matter is that in order to maintain a change; to actually stick to it is bloody difficult. I'd be lying if I said I didn't know people that are a lot more consistent than me when it comes to being able to make the sort of efforts to maintain what is needed to be constantly doing enough physically, however I'm pretty sure that even they slip from time to time.

This is just what happens and to I think it's important that we know that it's okay. In fact, if you take it to the extreme level, if you actually look at these proper health fanatics (thinking Lizzie from TV-AM, Mr Motivator from GMTV or Joe Wicks from GMB[17], as healthy as they might look and be, I bet they are boring as fuck to hang out with.

Whilst all of this bollocks I have been spouting is mainly based on my own experiences, and despite my various failings in leading a healthy life, the reality is that I know that compared to others I do actually do a lot more than most. This is why I think that I have so much sympathy for when I see people who are running who quite clearly not the type of person that has ever been someone that actually does this. This is a person that through 20

17 Covered 80's, 90's and present for wider audience reach

odd years of living in sedentary bliss are now panicking and feel compelled to suddenly start showing the world that they mean business by running down a road wearing Lycra that is too small and huffing and puffing and looking close to drawing their last breath.

This is not to mock the efforts; in fact I hold nothing but the upmost respect for anyone that decides to embark on this as it is not easy. The fact that this happens though is symptomatic of how we are conditioned to partake in this, especially as you get older. Suddenly the stakes are higher and the opportunity of avoidance is laden with risk. It's either get off your arse and do something or deteriorate and die. Thems your choices, you enjoy it.

The debate around health is the classic clash of objectivity vs subjectivity. The problem is that it is incredibly difficult to disseminate what might be legitimately objective e.g. you need to take this medication or you will die against what might be legitimately subjective e.g. someone telling you to take paracetamol for a headache when you could find a number of alternatives, or eat these types of foods etc.

It's easy to understand why, especially now with so much 'messaging' that what you end up with is a case of extremities, i.e. someone possibly pushing themselves too far or someone with nothing but contempt and deciding to do even more of the fuck all variety. In between is probably where we should be, but we do sail close to the wind on both fronts regardless.

As with all things, again it's about striking the right balance, although the caveat is that I think it is undisputed, or at least it should be, that we have to accept that as part of getting older, if we do want to have the chance of increasing our mortality, there has to be a compromise as to making enough life style changes that contribute towards, or increase the odds of this happening.

I do have this theory that for a lot of men, they often fall victim to believing there are only 2 paths available to them and this is based on either being single or being married, with partner etc.

Path 1 is to basically try and live the life that they always have. For men who are single, it is easy to believe (by mainly being generally consistent or unchanging), that you can go week to week doing whatever you were doing when you were 20. It might be for example, someone who drinks at different points of the week, gets to the weekend, drinks more, eats shit, and their only form of exercise might only be playing a game of football on a Saturday. You can often spot these guys when you are out. They will be the ones wearing the same leather jacket that they have worn for the last 20 years and could easily pass as a drummer that possibly was in Status Quo.

For men that are married, partnered (especially with kids), path 2 is to possibly emulate aspects of path 1 for a period of time, but due to other commitments then results in sporadic moments of physical exertion such as kicking a plastic ball 20 feet in the air, pushing a small bike, or carrying lots of shit. Other than that, it is a life of mainly drinking, eating loads of unhealthy food and generally sitting around watching Police shows and several news channels. You can often spot these people as they will most likely be wearing clothes that their partner has bought for them, will appear like they have just woken up, and possibly could have been a roadie for Status Quo.

I'm definitely projecting here slightly[18], but again, in many ways it is understandable why this occurs. There is a lot to be said as to how we are creatures of habit and how this plays into the impact it has on us making healthier decisions. This refers back to an element of contentment and in real terms from a health perspective you could argue that this is actually positive towards our mental health. Sure, we might get a bit pissed off at times by doing the same thing week to week, however, overall, we are content.

I imagine this is fairly similar for women as well in as much that the point I am making is that because of a belief that we have familiarity in what we do, we convince ourselves that this is what we should always do. Sure, you can factor in the various half arsed attempts to do make a concerted effort to do something different, however more often than not it amounts to very little.

Path 3 is only really an acceptance that path 1 and 2 don't really work. It's accepting that making a change

18 Okay, a lot

requires effort and it is likely to be both challenging and will mean that you may have to make certain sacrifices that could result in possibly seeing your life change in ways that might be difficult. Not difficult because you can't do it, difficult because it will be different. It could even mean that there is indeed a risk that this might make you even more miserable than you already are.

I'm almost certainly coming across as preachy and its possible that in this section I am probably projecting more than I should be. I just think that there is a lot to be said as to how exacerbating this is, yet at the same time there is a necessary evil here that has to be addressed, especially when you consider the objectivity vs subjectivity aspects of health.

The question that we need to ask, is this.

Whilst it is true that we could indeed get run over by a bus tomorrow, do we want to get run over and possibly end up on a slab looking like someone that has an affiliation with Status Quo?

This is indeed a rather convoluted wanky entry. Hopefully it makes sense in part, although it is likely it is a bit all over the fucking shop. Ultimately people have to make their own choices as to which direction they wish to go in. For some in might be small steps, others it could be going to extreme lengths. Either way, it's about wanting to do it, sticking to it and making sure it doesn't make you feel miserable.

Just to conclude though, here are some of the things that I have realised in recent years are:

1. Having an outdoor dog is amazing. It forces you to go for a walk in all weather. Pop on a good podcast or crack out an old music album. It keeps you fit and clears your head.[19]
2. Go and visit a swimming pool. This is great, not necessary for swimming, but realising that people come in all shapes and sizes.[20] You'll know that you are okay.
3. Visit a care home. This is a very humble experience where you get an insight into your future, whilst acknowledging your own ignorance in making the most of time we have, and also realising how pathetic you are at spending more time with the older members of your family.

I'm now going to eat some cakes, have a cry and do 100 press ups. At the same time I shall listen to 'Rockin all over the world'.

---

19 Despite several cigarettes being had
20 Not in a pervy way of course

Technology

I've got mixed feelings about technology. I wouldn't claim to be someone that gets particularly excited about it, in as much that I would never, and have never, been enthused enough about new technology coming out, with the belief that it's going to drastically change my life. My relationship with it though is that I am aware of it, and when there is an opportunity to engage with it, I'll often do so. I will then either decide to include it in my life, or to make mockery of those that have, especially when I believe it to be shit. If I can't use it, I have therefore determined it is shit and is only used by complete dickheads.[21]

I accept that as of late this often results in me having bouts of tech excitement, which then leads to me enthusing this to others (mainly my wife and kids), only to be met with a response which quite rightly points out to the fact that they are already using said technology, and that I am just a luddite and tight, with strong inferences being made to my age and lack of funds.[22]

It is this though that I think adds or creates this myth that technology is something that is only for the young, or at least only understood by them. It is easy to see why this is the perception that most people would have, although if you think about it, what we are really talking about is more

---

21 See Bluetooth earpieces circa early 2000's

22 Direct references

to do with ‘new technology’. Our relationship with it is something that I would argue is at its peak when we are young as our exposure to it is that much greater, largely because to an extent there is a conformity or expectancy that we must embrace it because it it’s seen as crucial towards our first steps of ‘fitting in’. This is not a new phenomenon, as much as we might want to criticise the effects of technology in our world today, the fact is that at the heart of this, the push back is more to do with our reluctance to move away from the technologies that have become part of how we live our lives. This is either because we know it will be expensive, and equally (and most importantly), we know it will be a ballache to get our heads around.

A lot of this refers back to some of the points that I addressed when looking at nostalgia, in many ways our relationship with technology is defined by that which we are subjected to at whatever time we are born. If I consider the things that I grew up with, there are two ways of looking at this. In order to do this though, it is important to list the various technologies which should in theory make this an easy task. For some people (assuming people are actually reading this), it will resonate more, whilst others will probably have to do a google search.

In no particular order:

Atari 2600

Walkman (tape and CD variety)

VHS
Tomytronic (the tank one)
Calculators (solar)
Commodore 64
Hi-Fi (double tape deck)
Casio watch (with in-built calculator)
Megadrive
DVD player

I think for anyone who is the same age as me, or there or thereabouts, I would assume that the feelings towards these items are likely to be the same. As to the 'two ways' of looking at these, in the first instance, my own and I suspect other's initial reaction is one of fondness because we can relate specifically to our interactions with them both on a personal level and socially with others. Whilst to an extent we can agree that on a purely functional level they did the job they were made to do, the second way we view them is that there were a number of times these were shit. Sure, I liked playing a game on the Commodore 64, I just hated waiting a week for the damn game to load up. Likewise, I liked listening to my Walkman, however I didn't like the tape getting chewed up and was always a bit miffed when the batteries started to run down, and with it the song I was listening to.[23][24]

---

23 Maybe this was how the Kylie/Rick Astley thing was discovered

24 Obscure as fuck reference

I think these examples though are fairly indicative of all technology through the ages. I'm stating the obvious, but it really is just taking something as it is, and just pursuing a route to making a better version of it. Everything I listed here is culmination or just a moment in time where these were the methods of delivery for things that we have always had as humans, in one form another. Whether it be music, being entertained by others, playing games or even doing maths. Any technical advances made, at their base level, are just about making things either a 'bit' better, or a possibly a 'lot' better. And just like everything on the list, they often are considered initially to be good, but at some point, then become shit.

The reason that it is important to recognise this, is because it probably offers either the best hope of a more homogenous relationship between generations, not necessarily because you have to embrace the same tools and use them in the same way, but it is wrong to simply dismiss it (and them in the process), leading to more of a divide.

I think the concern that most people who reach a certain age have with technology is more to do with the rate of change that it is delivered to us. It is precisely because of what technology was available for a period of time that defines our understanding, or labelling of generations. If we look at how many generations we now recognise, and those that co-exist because we are all living longer, there is a real chance that we will become quite fragmented. More than we currently are already. We should though see it as an opportunity for it possibly to be crucial towards people reaching the consensus that we don't actually want, or need as much technology as we are conditioned to believe we do. There are those, and I include myself, that there is an increasing demand towards this, a kind of reverse technology revolution as people get to the point where they long for a simpler life. We just need to be careful of how this might be achieved. You would hope that collectively people of all ages are more accepting of that in some areas we probably don't have to pursue some technology so aggressively and instead push it towards being developed on those things that we should be more concerned with.

There are so many ills in the world where technology could or should be used, yet it often seems that because of the focus that we put on economic growth, most efforts by companies and even governments are mainly trying to appeal to consumerism.

It is this that forms at least some of the debate. Some will argue that it is through the technical advances made in recent years that have contributed towards making progress in offering better alternatives, that will indeed positively impact the wider society. This can be evidenced in what has been achieved in how we have seen how we now place greater emphasis on technology for the environment. The problem though is even something that is 'good', it is still laced in consumerism being the trigger or the main reason why these things happen. It is not until this is deemed to be practical or cost effective to drive this on to deliver the benefits that they should bring. For me, this is the wrong way to approach how technology is developed. I appreciate it might not be the responsibility of businesses to do this on their own, and certainly for the bigger stuff, it shouldn't have to be, it should be governments.

I'm kmow this is coming across as overtly political, which it is, however I can't help but think that we should be pissed off if there is a lack of real action because we accept it to be the norm that we can allow inequality with how technology is made available. It is precisely because of this that we then have inequalities in other areas which both directly, indirectly and fucking bizarrely, seems to all feed back towards more of an incessant demand for consumerism. Imagine if we put as much focus on giving everyone (and I mean absolutely fucking everyone), the means to benefit from technology that will help them. I'm not talking about ensuring everyone has the latest iPhone, so they can get right on Instagram, I'm referring specifically to anything that will contribute to betterment of lives at the basic levels of need. This might be housing, heating, eating etc. Perhaps if we were to switch our focus, or our demands so that this is attended to, we might be less bothered about newer ways that technology might push us further apart from one another?

I must admit that when I initially planned to write about technology, I didn't expect to go off on such a tangent. I believe I was going to provide a number of examples as to how my own experiences have been with it. I think though that I probably needed to get that off my chest as there is a lot to be said and not just to consider the topic to be about technology that is just there to make us feel more equipped on helping us entertain ourselves. For most people, I think is would be this which would be where they go to when giving their opinions. It is interesting that they will base this on their relationship with it from this perspective.[25]

It is the 'communicative' aspect which is often cited when extolling the benefits of the tools we use today as to how we are now living in a world that is able to communicate more effectively than ever before. This message began once we had the internet thrust upon us, and in fairness, at the very beginning there was a sense of true enthusiasm as well as optimism that this was going to revolutionise our ability to gain knowledge. It is worth noting that the communication part was limited to email and really nothing else. Interestingly though, my memories of this period are that the true beauty of how we used this initially, still meant that it was almost an extra-curricular activity. It wasn't something that you necessarily had immediate access to as we do today, it was much more of a process, akin to visiting a library, but basically doing this from a computer in your home, or for a lot of people, at school or an actual library itself.

25 Massive fucking assumption.

There was also a lot to be said about CD-ROMs at this time. These were being peddled out relentlessly to entice us in to learn about all sorts of things via the computer. Encarta was the one that was a must have, released yearly with new and exciting facts about things that had been readily available in books for years.

There was an innocence at this time as to what we now had access to; by this I mean that it was exciting to be able to suddenly have this technology at our disposal. Crucially though, which I think is significant, is that as an activity this was something that was quite separate from our general interactions in our social settings. Certainly, it was not as intrusive as it is today, it was much more something that we did on our own, and although it was still often anti-social, it wasn't necessarily ignorant in the same way as we view it today. It was the start however of our appetite for more consumption of what was being offered.

Ultimately, it has been the development of both computers, the internet and phones which has culminated in the world as we know it today. To take something that was initially an 'activity' or something that we tended to do on our own, to where it is something that we do all the time, is a significant jump in 20 years. For young people, the scary thing is that is all they have ever known, and when coupled with an increase in selective reading, viewing etc which is quite individualistic, it is no wonder that division is as high as it is right now. We have allowed this to happen as we have somehow reasoned that we must live our lives in such a way where we are plugged in to everything and everyone.

A lot of this is obvious and even as I type this, I am aware that all I am doing is feeding into the stereotypical 'old person' moaning about a longing for how things used to be better in the olden days. There is definitely some truth to this, but not in the way that is intended to misrepresent or blame technology. In many ways I'm quite envious of what younger people have available to them today, and I often wonder how if given the same access to what they have, what difference this may have made in my life. I like to imagine that I would have been much more inclined to try and explore my creative side, although equally I do concede that there is also an increased likelihood that I would have got in more trouble than I already did without it!

As with anything, we can only gauge this through our own experiences, and all I would say (mainly through my interaction or lack of it) with my own kids as to being left with a feeling that the family dynamic is undermined. There are of course levels to this, but I imagine in most households today, there is a distinct disconnect as unlike yesteryear, where there socially as a family we were mostly all exposed to the same things. Today, it is not uncommon for mum to be on Facebook, dad to be trawling through YouTube, son to be gaming, and daughter to be fixated on

TikTok[26] . The reality is that it is because we have elected to open ourselves up to this way of life, which we justify because we feel that we should have the right to entertain ourselves as we see fit, means that the further the path we go down, the more we perceive this to be normal. Skip forward and remove any checks and balances i.e. parents limiting time on devices[27], then it is not inconceivable that children will just be brought up by apps.

It was not my intention to be as down on technology as I have come across as I realise that a lot of what I have written might suggest that I have Amish tendencies. I can assure you that it was not my intention to be as negative as I have been. I'm actually quite hypocritical in a lot of what I have said, I think it is mainly because part of me is frustrated because I have found myself being susceptible to the ills of technology, especially with regards to the lure of social media and how this distorts our reality.

I don't know what the answer is, but I do know that if the next 20 years are as rapid as the previous 20, then I suspect that we should brace ourselves for the possibility that we are more removed from one another, which is ironic given the fact that we were told it would bring us closer together.

---

26 Revealing stuff eh

27 As if that fucking works

Annoyances

I began writing this chapter about 5 weeks ago because at the time, upon arriving at writing about annoyances, I found myself at that particular moment stuck with not having enough things to talk about. This is not to say that there weren't any, it was just that right there and then, my brain was unable to tap into the right mindset, which more often than not (about 78%), results in me questioning the point of pretty much everything. This is not to say that I'm living in this perpetual state which means I'm mostly angry, as when it comes to my interpretation of annoyances, what actually annoys me is sub-divided into various categories, with the vast majority being that which I readily accept would constitute as being trivial. Neither is this related to my age, as this is something that I believe has always been with me.

There is a lot to be said regarding the relationship with the things that we learn (useful and bollocks varieties), and the amount of what we learn. If you then add the state of our minds and particular circumstances that we find ourselves in, I believe that these are the determining factors as to not only what we choose to bitch and moan about but also the extent or amount that we then try to inflict onto others, as we feebly attempt to ‘win them over’.

I don’t want to conflate ‘annoyances’ necessarily with the strength of opinions that people might have on what might be considered to be serious, such as politics, religion etc, as I think that it is important to differentiate or consider exactly what constitutes as annoying over that which we are vehement about. I readily accept that this is extremely difficult to do as the issue is that when you try to apply this from a collective viewpoint, the problem clearly becomes challenging, because whether we like it or not, once again we are afflicted by the perils of subjectivity, which becomes abundantly clear when we find ourselves playing our part in the wider society.

Clearly then, whilst on a personal level it is conceivable that it is possible to apply your own standards or understanding as to the difference between what you should, or can be ‘annoyed’ about; which on face value is mainly trivial vs that which we should be ‘annoyed’ about, because its really fucking important that we do. The question is whether or not it is possible that we can reach consensus that the word ‘annoying’ should only be applied to certain things. If, for example, should we have an opinion on something that we wish to share with others, perhaps prior to commencing with such opinion, should we inform the receiver of our imminent thoughts, that we have properly made it clear as to the validity or seriousness of what we are about to say. If we then proceed, perhaps if we did this, it could result in a much more harmonious and greater respect of such opinions being treated with the respect that they deserve.

Of course, all of what I have just said both poorly explained and is utter bollocks, however I believe that this is has been a valid and valiant effort to properly set out those things that I consider to be 'annoyed' about, as opposed to anything else that I am mega fucking fucking pissed off about.

Here is a picture

Annoyed———————————————MFFPOA[28]

Hopefully, this diagram that I have called 'Clarkes annoyance scale', might help in now reintroducing my previous work that this period of reflection has allowed me to provide this edited introduction. By now looking at what will be some examples of things that bother me, I now feel more comfortable that by now inserting my initial previous 5 weeks ago work, enough context has been applied so that by the end of this chapter it will be easy to understand the purpose of my 'annoyances' and how they personally affect me. I will use my scale to identify the importance of my thought on said annoyance. (end edit)

---

28 Mega Fucking Fucking Pissed Off About

It is vital that I begin by listing as many things that I find annoying at this moment in time (insert edit – this was Christmas 2021). (end last edit) This is not a complete list and neither is it any particular order. Each one will be provided with a reason, which may be brief or longish. These are all my own opinions and should be considered or treated as 'mega fucking important'. (Okay, final final edit, I've just realised that I have contradicted my own logic and thus possibly renders everything that I have said as of Christmas 2021 as a reflection of the difference that can occur to a person over 1 month).[29]

The Omaze Advert and (that woman)

Firstly, I admit that my initial problem is particularly with regards to this 'competition' which is targeted at people trying to make the idea of having loads of posh shit as 'aspirational'. To enter this, you have to buy a ticket or something similar, which you then stand a chance to win. As to the odds of winning, as per their website it says "The odds of winning depend on the number of entries received."[30] (which whilst this is correct, I do believe it still warranted some figurative examples), and additionally, the woman who is in the adverts appears fake. Very fake and very posh.

29 What a complete cunt I am
30 https://omaze.co.uk/pages/faqs

As for elaborating further, I will try. I have no problem ‘per se’ with people wanting to have a lifestyle which may incorporate elements of what is suggested in the adverts; however I find it all a bit dystopian based on how it’s all quite reminiscent of the film ‘Elysium’. Think about it. People are being sold this idea of how they can step out of the shit they are in and have this lavish lifestyle. That’s the entire plot of Elysium apart from the fact that they were not necessarily sold the chance to go to Elysium as directly as in the Omaze adverts, and although they kind of had to get a ticket (through much criminal-based activities), unlike Omaze where you just buy one, the overall message is the same. ‘Up here its fucking ace, come and see’. As for my problem with the woman, much of this is to do with how she delivers the advert. I don’t find that she is being sincere and is quite resentful about the possibility of someone who is not ‘typical’ to the environment that she is advocating is indeed amazing, or in this instance ‘omazing’. I find it quite unsettling.

These are the main reasons for my apathy, although in combination mode (lavish + posh + fake), I believe it only reinforces my continued contempt to all that is ‘materialistic’.

Calendars/Diaries/Schedules

One thing I have noticed over the last 10 years is an increased use of my friends constantly referring to ‘checking diaries’, whenever a proposal is made towards any sort of congregation, it is met with the immediate response of having to check with one of the above.

I suppose the thing that I mostly have a problem with is not the fact that there will indeed be pre-arranged events that one of my friends have committed to, it’s the fact that this has been written down somewhere. It is that for me I find, for whatever reason, to be contrived. As to why, it is mainly because not only do I find it personally strange (with the exception of a holiday), to be in a position where your life is so planned in advance that it somehow makes you a sort of prisoner of your time. The idea that not only do you write these future events down, but you end up with this document of sorts that dictates where or what you will be doing and you are bound by it. Whenever I hear the words ‘I’ll have to check my diary’, the immediate go to thought is that the person informing me of their intention to do this, is that they are wankers by virtue of the fact that they have such a high opinion of themselves that they need to see whether they could possibly accommodate little old me.

It’s not actually the fact that I can’t accept that people will have other commitments, however, outside of the world of holidays, the fact that people have to check, or can check what they will be doing in 3 months and 2 days on a Tuesday, results in me having nothing but pure apathy towards them.

Perhaps this is reflection of my own limited social activities, however I believe that I do have a fairly busy life. It's probably more likely that I think that if you step towards retirement age, where you combine this with full blown itineraries. That and the fact that this is something that I know is mainly thrust upon married/partnered men by their wives/girlfriends.

Illnesses

Annoyed---MFFPOA

I am convinced that I don't get ill, so much so that although I can recollect periods of time where I have been unwell that it is so infrequent that I now don't consider them as actual bouts of illness, based on the fact that I struggle to recollect the feeling of being ill. Whilst this makes no sense, the reality is that it has created a complete void of empathy towards anyone who is ill. Obviously, I am not referring to any debilitating illnesses that could result in loss of life, I am mainly referring to anything that might fall into the category of mild illnesses, such as coughs, colds and headaches etc.

I think most of my resentment is predominantly based on the subjectivity of these types of illnesses, where the truth as to the actual pain or difficulty that one of these ailments has on those apparently afflicted, is ridiculously grey. I can say with 100% honesty that at that exact moment where I have been informed of said illness, either directly from the individual, or by others, automatically I have formed an immediate dismissive view of this. Naturally, and out of courtesy I am aware enough to present an empathic response, especially towards the individual, however inside I am being very judgmental, and if truth be known I'm thinking 'yeah yeah, whatever'.

Given the opportunity to be told the news of another person's illness, all bets are now off, which often means I get to vent my spleen and start banging on about hypochondria and Munchausen syndrome. I also think about days I have worked and days they haven't and I end up firmly in the camp that the true illness here is that I have been wronged and these people are taking the piss.

Other things (without any rating being applied)

- Cars (When they break and you know fuck all about what is going on and being told car jargon to explain how you suddenly need to spend shit loads of money on that you don't have)

- The National Lottery (when all the pompous bollocks was going on with the naming if machines and the guy in the white gloves and being told ball 29 has been drawn over 488 times since the draw started in 1994)

- Adverts (any advert that has a classic song that is slowed down and recorded by a young girl – used all the fucking time by lazy marketing folk)

- Horse people (no explanation given)

There are definitely a lot more of these that I could easily spend time moaning about, but like all of the above, the fact of the matter is that all this really does is highlight the sheer randomness of it all and this is the problem with annoyances. We find ourselves getting consumed, or drawn in by stuff that at best is humourous, but at worst just takes us further way from the ability to be more at peace with things.

To top it off though, the most annoying thing about all this 'annoying bollocks' is that sadly I don't think there is anything that can actually be done to remedy this, even if we make a concerted effort to try and not give a fuck about any of it, there is an internal trigger that just sets us off which then means we spend sometimes an inordinate amount of time bitching about it to anyone who we think might equally feel as vexed as we do about it. The only real possible way out of this that I can see, is if we physically remove ourselves from everything and everyone. Then and only then could we be confident that we are less likely to be subjected to those things that are inadvertently going to piss us off. Even then there is the risk that we might find something shit about nothing.

The reason bringing this up though, as with my earlier point as to the scale or real differences over what annoys us, and what we truly feel passionate about, I think we have an increasing inability to apply true context to whatever it is we are exposed to. Even if we accept the stark differences that exist between that which mildly frustrates us, against that which we genuinely feel aggrieved by, the reality is that for the majority of us, when it comes to how much effort we apply to both, we will spend more time consumed by shit that we shouldn't be consumed by.

I have definitely made more of this than I initially intended to, I guess I'm taking the view, or line as to trying to emphasise how much we take for granted our privilege that we find ourselves in, especially in Western societies, that we are fortunate to have lives where we can afford not only the finer luxuries provided to us, yet despite this fortuitous position, we spend an inordinate amount of time hell bent on banging on about, or being fixated on things that really don't matter.

There is something here that makes sense, I think. It might have been easier if I just summarised this in a small paragraph in an earlier chapter. Then again, I was so fucking annoyed, I just had to put it out there.

Resistance is futile?

For starters, should this be, 'Is resistance futile?' As I have no fucking idea.

I suppose the title would suggest that I am making more of a statement, as opposed to raising a question, however is there a rule that allows the insertion of a question mark on top of a statement, that is deemed permissible without being grammatically incorrect? I really don't fucking know, and now because I have this doubt over the title, I'm now thinking about the association of this reference to this phrase cited in Star Trek the Next Generation TV show (1987-1994)[31], which to those that do not know, refers to a cyborg based, technologically dominant aggressive species. So aggressive in fact and true of their own convictions, that it's not enough to offer others the chance to see what it's all about; they insist upon completely changing other species by assimilating them into them. It's all quite complex really, especially if you have never seen Star Trek. Even if you have, there is a lot more going on at both a

31 Excluded movies as more prominent in series

metaphorical and societal level, that leaves a lot to unpick. None more so indeed as to the question or statement, that 'Resistance is indeed futile'.

Now I've got that out of the way, I would like to share something about where I currently am as to this book, and in many ways, this is quite poignant as to the title of this chapter.

As of now, I feel a mix of contentment and fear. Contentment because there is a reality to being close to achieving something, with this book taking centre stage. I don't know if there is a link here to other things/responsibilities that I have going on in my life, but this also appears to be catching and I appear to be taking a different view on those things which is making me feel more in control of them. Equally though, there is a degree of fear that kicks in whenever this happens, because for me, there is this immediate built-in sense of failure. Not through want or effort of avoidance, but more so that for whatever fucking reason, something will inevitably go wrong.

There is a lot to be said about perspective, as I do accept that it can often be easy to conspire in a belief that everyone, or everything is out to get us, especially when things don't go our way. The problem is though, that it's quite the thing to perhaps be philosophical in the face of adversity, although as admirable this might be, whether it something that is sustainable is another matter.

The reason I wanted to share this is because in doing so, I think that this reflects the essence of futility. As negative as this might sound, this is not necessarily a bad thing, it's much more about readily accepting that it's perfectly okay to enjoy whatever moments of happiness or contentment that you might have, it's just that equally we must accept that there is a futility to how long this might last.

The real question though is whether there is any merit in trying to push back, not just when it comes to this but on other things as well? If say for example, is it a case that we must accept that in the fullness of time that we will wear chinos on a daily basis, should we make proactive moves to embrace or avoid? Should we continue to walk past allotments confident in the fact that the people that use them are all a bit weird, vowing never to want to have a small plot of land to grow beetroot, light fires and read old pornographic magazines in sheds? Is it actually the case that whether we like it or not, this will be somehow be our destiny?

Clearly, I am asking a lot of hypothetical questions, or possibly I'm making wild assertions about an inevitability as to what we might expect. It's not necessarily advocating that we should conform to this, yet at the same time I'm wondering whether there is more sense in naturally embracing those things that we are expected to, simply because it is easier to do this than to push back As silly as this sounds, in part we have always been doing this, gravitating towards those things/pursuits/interests that we have convinced ourselves is what is best for us. This is not to say that we have not been without free choice as to making decisions as to that which we choose to do, however it is my view that those same freedoms are more diminished as we get older and conventionally there is greater impetus towards being at least seen to making a concerted effort to fit into certain categories and by proxy allow ourselves to become a stereotype of sorts.

I'll try to explain this further. In order to do so though, the best way to understand is to strip it down to the basics, and view this from the position of the collective and not the individual.

If we forget about, or remove any personal interests that we might have, and view our participation in the wider society, (especially as a couple or as a nuclear 2.4 child family), it is easier to begin to recognise that in order to essentially fit in, there are a number of things that we must be doing, or at least be seen as wanting to do. In order to demonstrate this, it is important to consider exactly what these things are and then talk around each one. As before with other lists, these are in no particular order, but remember though, it is important to not confuse this with our personal interests, although there could arguably be some overlap depending on what these are.

Holidays

We must have a holiday, some of us must have 2 or 3, some of us must go abroad, some of us must go to Devon and some of us must go on a cruise and some of us must go camping in France. Obviously, there is nothing wrong with wanting a holiday as it is an opportunity to give ourselves a break from the mundanity of wherever it is that we have come to resent, so it makes perfect sense to go away to somewhere else for a while. The problem I have with this though is that when it comes to our choices, whilst there are limitations as to what our choices are, mainly due to financial constraints, it doesn't change the fact that once we determine what money we have at our disposal we then either knowingly or unknowingly become part of a wider group of people who are all doing the same fucking thing.

As to how this relates to futility, the point is that on one hand because of financial limitations, there is an acceptance that we must therefore do whatever (which isn't much) because that's all we can do. On the flip side though and where I think this falls down, is that even if we are not financially restrained, people still are conditioned, accepting or wanting to belong to a particular group of people that do exactly the same thing. Think about it, if you have a shit load of money, do you go to a camp site in Devon still? I think not. Going back is not only an undesired option, in fact it is considered a downright failure.

It's as if there is an equation or formula that sets out what we should do based on a set of conditions or circumstances that we find ourselves in, and it is this that I have begun to really understand and consider to be futile. It's as if that regardless of whether I want to or not I am sure at one stage I will be in the position to afford to go to Centreparcs and also go on a fucking cruise[32]. As of now, I have zero interest in either of these, however part of me already knows that at some point there will be a picture of me on a mountain bike with all my family wearing matching Cagoules, smiling near some wooded bridge. And in the fullness of time I'll also be in a picture wearing an aertex top, tucked into some chinos, at a bar on a ship next to a very tanned man drinking a cocktail that I don't like with multiple neon straws protruding into my face.

This is just one example which everyone can relate to, we like to think this is about personal choice, but it really isn't, this is social conditioning based on doing what we should be doing based on what we earn and the company we keep. A conformity of convenience. A kind of wank version of Total Recall.

Houses

I want to make it clear that there is nothing wrong with wanting a house, in fact, it is something that is can easily be argued that it should be viewed as essential, at least in

---

32 I know I have mentioned these before, I do really despise them both

terms of having a roof over our heads and somewhere which we can call home.

Like holidays though, there is something about houses that I consider to have aspects of futility with regards to how they impact our lives, or how we succumb or fall victim to them as to both what we must do as minimum in terms of upkeep, and what we do with them as to how we choose to present it to others (showing off). The futility is that when it comes to what we do with our houses, we know that there are certain duties or requirements that we should fulfill as a matter of course, such as decorating, having carpets, mowing the lawn etc etc, and whilst there is an acceptance, or indeed a level of some pride that is reasonable, the more we entertain these mandatory obligations, the more we start to readily become a little bit too preoccupied or obsessed with a pursuit of wanting to make our houses become both a reflection of our personalities and a depiction of our social status. This is especially true for those who believe that this adds further value to their property and then equate this to some sort of paper form of wealth that they use to justify their extravagances. Whilst there may indeed be some of this that it done under duress (husband/wife dynamic), whatever way you cut it, there is clearly a desire to demonstrate to others that you either have what they have, or have something that they don't and that they to should aspire to have.[33]

---

33 This excludes hoarders

There is a line in the movie ‘Fight Club’ where the lead character Tyler Durden comments “The things you own, end up owning you”, and for me, this has always resonated, although equally I have found myself falling victim to this sentiment. Sure, it is possible to acknowledge the logic here and the idea that we should be more attentive to the ‘little pleasures’ that life offers, however the reality is that it’s an ideological position that most of us are incapable of following. Hence, the futility again is on full display as it’s something that we all do, in my case with a degree of self-loathing, but for others a degree of self-brilliance.

Retirement

Although I still have a considerable amount of time left in the world of work, in recent years it has become clear that not only will this become reality faster than I envisage it, but also it requires a bit more attention than I have ever given it before. And for what reason? So that upon finishing my employment that I might have enough money to sustain or maintain whatever standard of life that I have become accustomed to having.

For me, this is the epitome of futility, the idea that we must focus or start to put money aside for a life that we may or may not have, for a future that we have no assurances over and to partake in things that we probably don’t even like. Is this an oversimplification? Absolutely. However, there is a reality to this, and again, as to what type of retirement we might look forward to is pretty much dictated by or mirrored by whatever life we are living at present. Sure, it is possible that circumstances can change for the good, or indeed there can be greater efforts made in the way of investment that could result in a retirement that may offer you more than you might have had prior to this, however, by it's definition being able to retire is merely to provide you with the financial equivalences to what you have been accustomed to having whilst you were working. The 'bonus' if there is any, is now instead of being at work, you can now rest easy and do all those things that you like to do in your spare time, but even more.

What scares me most is currently in my spare time, whilst there is indeed a lot that I do which I enjoy, there is a lot of what I do which is pretty pointless and quite wasteful. Having the commitment of actually having to go to work, of which as previously highlighted is where we spend the vast majority of time, offers at the very least a sense of purpose. The idea that this then gets removed and I'm provided with more time to do a lot more of nothing, fills me with dread. Even more so, if the argument is that, instead of doing nothing I can look forward to taking up golf, gardening, having a daily pint of bitter in some grotty pub, getting free bus rides, or god fucking forbid, going on cruises[34]. Either way, it's not really that appealing.

If you throw into the mix the added likelihood that you have 10 years of doing this, before being shipped off to a

34 No further mentions after this

care home that you then have to sell your home to afford, then it's all rather bleak.

Of course, I'm being quite facetious, but fundamentally the point I am making is that there is a lot to be said as to how even if we believe we are living our lives as independently as we think we are, there is a degree to everything that we do where we are merely ticking certain boxes. It doesn't necessarily equate to not having any self-fulfillment or not being able to feel like we are in control, it just raises the question as to why we are conditioned, or convinced that this is what we must do in order to so that we have some sense of purpose.

So, does this mean that everything ultimately is futile? I guess in part it does, certainly if everyone is as negative about is as I am. In truth though, regardless as to what I have said, the reality is that we don't, or shouldn't be compelled to view these parts of our lives in such a way that makes it futile. It is our inability or fear in breaking from convention that only results in us missing the good bits. If we lose sight of this and focus our efforts on merely only doing what we are expected to do, then not only are we not resisting, but we are openly embracing futility.

The beginning of the end

I'm here, I really am.

I have pictured this in my mind, in fact, at one point in writing this book, given that I was unconvinced in my ability to do this, I contemplated writing the final chapter earlier on and possibly having this as an additional appendices, assuming of course that by the time I actually got here, that whatever I would have written previously would not have made as much sense, due to the fact that it would have been a lot of pre-amble based on an assumption of what I think the final chapter would have been about. As opposed to the final chapter being a reflection of the everything that I have experienced in constructing this book. All in all it appeared good at the time, but as per most things, I convinced myself it was a shit idea.

Part of me though is a little disappointed that I didn't do this, as from memory, when I was thinking about doing it, my energy levels and general focus was considerably better than where it is right now. In all likelihood it probably would have been far superior than what I will now write.

One of the most challenging aspects, but equally rewarding part of this journey is that despite at times calling into question the quality of my writing, or indeed the lack of a coherent structure, and a shit load of repetition, the more that I wrote, the less I cared. Perhaps, given my aspirations to write something that people might actually like, or to pursue avenues to have this published, it could well be that I have failed on both accounts, but in order to finish this, I needed to have this attitude, otherwise I would have spent ages procrastinating. Whilst this is most likely that I have failed with respect to the above, overall, I have mostly stayed true to why I decided to write this in the first place. I did it for me and to prove that I could do it, and in doing so perhaps provide a little inspiration for others to dare to try. Even if the end product is not particularly great, it's still something that is complete and, in many ways, that's what it's all about. Anything we do could always be done better, but sometimes it's when we do something for the first time that we learn the most.

Assuming that you have read this book, firstly thank you, and secondly I would like to think that regardless as to whether you have agreed or disagreed with my assertions or views on life, I would hope that at the minimum I have demonstrated, or conveyed my thoughts and feelings on the various subject matters that I have raised. I do not profess that I am necessarily right on anything that I have said, but I do know that everything is indeed 'my truth', so that must count for something right?

I know I am an overthinker, crucially though, and because of choosing to write about this, I have discovered that it is not necessarily such a bad affliction to have. When we overthink, the worst aspects of this are that we often decide to keep our thoughts to ourselves, through fear of sharing or saying something that might be construed as confirmation that we are not quite right. For those of us that find ourselves consumed with thoughts that take us all over the place, it can be difficult to not only make sense of what we think, but also find peace with it as in many ways it can often feel relentless and never ending. Through the process of writing, even if as evidenced those thoughts are a bit disjointed, by virtue of that fact that it is written down, it goes some way in taking the noise levels down in your brain. It was, and is a very cathartic outlet, something that is incredibly cliché, however, both true and highly recommended as a partial cure.

So, did I break any of the rules that I set for myself and what have I learnt?

Well, for starters, one of the biggest rules I broke was that from early on after completing some of the chapters, I did find myself re-reading what I had wrote which I discovered is pretty unavoidable, especially when you start to get into the flow of writing. I wouldn't say that this was a problem in as much that it didn't stop me from having the confidence to just put stuff out there, it just meant that once I had done this, I merely chose, or felt compelled to tidy certain parts up to try and make it as coherent as I could. As I have stated throughout, I am not convinced I have nailed this, however it is not for want of trying.

Another interesting aspect of this process was planning. I had this idea that I knew everything that I wanted to say and exactly how I would say it. Whilst there is some truth to this, the reality is that often even with the right intentions, or with notes that I had written down in preparation, I found that once I began writing, it was easier to just go off on a tangent. At first this was frustrating, however I began to realise that although this is probably not how it should be done, for me, it was how it must be done. I'm not entirely happy with this as, there are definitely some parts that I have written that are messy as fuck, but again, this was an important factor in being able to get through this, and crucially have this be my voice. I think certainly towards the end there is an argument to be had that 'less fucks are given', but at the same time there is an honesty that I wanted to get across. As lazy as this sounds (and it is), it is still true.

As for writing 273 pages? This was much harder than I thought it would be, not because it is impossible, but because I set myself a target to complete this in 6-8 months, It became clear that this was going to be too much of a challenge. When coupled with my own impatience and desperation to have this finished, I quickly arrived at the decision to revert to writing a 'novella'. Until researching what this was, it appeared to meet my criteria and that was fine by me. Additionally, I did think about enlarging the font to Arial 16, which would be one method towards getting closer to 273 pages, however, this is apparently not permitted. The one thing I would say though, is that given my latter disregard and new ability to ramble like a bastard, I would feel more encouraged to take on this task now, whereas upon seeing how many words this would be after writing 25 pages, the thought of trying to do this was extremely daunting. I'm pretty sure this was the exact moment that I decided I had to make some revisions to my plans for this book. It was here where a lot of doubt crept in, mainly due to my novice approach and because the frigging template suggested that this amount was 'normal'.

The one thing that I do now have which I did not at the start of this process, was a new found admiration for those that write as a profession. It's not enough to just have an idea or something that you want to write about, it's more than that, it's a commitment and a constant challenge. I understand more than ever that writing can become addictive, especially once you have begun the process of putting down all those things that what you want to say. The best thing about this is that there is an element of control over what you choose to do. Again, this is quite enlightening as you become empowered in your thoughts and with it comes a degree of increased confidence in being able to put this down to your hearts content. I am sure it might be comparable to writing a diary or a journal, however the intent in writing in a book for others to see changes the dynamic. It's not necessarily because anyone will read what you have written, but the words you choose, or ,what you are willing to part with takes on a different meaning, as to a certain extent as you are mindful of not just what you reveal, but how you need or choose to reveal it.

And this is what I have tried to do.

I accept wholeheartedly that I may have missed the mark, it could well be that everything I have said makes me come across as a bit narcissistic, deluded or both. Perhaps my interpretation of what it means to 'overthink' is misguided and it could well be that all I have done is manage to bleat on about all these things that suggest I'm just a bitter middle-aged man venting his spleen. And whilst I hope that I have not come across this way, equally I know that it is irrelevant. I need to not give a shit in order to make this happen. The whole point of putting yourself out there means that you must accept that you run the risk of criticism. In many ways regardless of what you choose to write about, it is something that you must accept is a likely outcome.

I don't know what I will do next, but I do know that having set myself this challenge it has provided me with a greater perspective of who I am and a new found confidence to take on whatever the world chooses to throw at me.

A long time ago, I was given a poem that has always resonated with me. What I took from it most was the phrase ‘*words are weak*’. I’ve always taken this as sacrosanct, fully aware of the magnitude and importance that it is what we do that will always trump anything that we say. I feel as strongly about this now as I did then. The only difference though is that that sometimes, what we say, or in this case, what we write, if said with honesty and with passion, might just go some way to be seen on an equal footing.

"Be Yourself"

Someone falls to pieces
Sleeping all alone
Someone kills the pain
Spinning in the silence
She finally drifts away

Someone gets excited
In a chapel yard
And catches a bouquet
Another lays a dozen
White roses on a grave

And to be yourself is all that you can do
To be yourself is all that you can do

Someone finds salvation in everyone
Another only pain
Someone tries to hide himself
Down inside himself he prays

Someone swears his true love

Until the end of time
Another runs away
Separate or united?
Healthy or insane?

And to be yourself is all that you can do
To be yourself is all that you can do
To be yourself is all that you can do
To be yourself is all that you can do

Even when you've paid enough
Been pulled apart or been held up
With every single memory of
The good or bad, faces of luck
Don't lose any sleep tonight
I'm sure everything will end up alright

You may win or lose

But to be yourself is all that you can do
To be yourself is all that you can do

Audioslave 2005

www.ingramcontent.com/pod-product-compliance
Ingram Content Group UK Ltd.
Pitfield, Milton Keynes, MK11 3LW, UK
UKHW041846190726
13854UKWH00002B/743

9 781471 752070